Zero Soles

Michael Jesse McLaughlin

Energy can neither be created nor destroyed; energy can only be transferred or changed from one form to another. - The first law of thermodynamics

CONTENTS

Intro

I started on this journey with the intention of challenging my beliefs of what is real. Since I came into this world, I had been told from others, my parents, teachers, friends, the internet, social media, and society in general what to value, what to fear, and how to spend my time in this existence.

My wish is that you may find inspiration to challenge your current beliefs and discover for yourself what is real and what is possible.

INTRO

I believe we all experience these moments at some point in our lives where we choose to go against logic, against what our brain is telling us. We ignore the voices and opinions of others and put our faith in something we can't explain. We listen to our heart – our gut instinct.

To boil it down, I observed that I had been living in an outdated system, with rules which do not have a foundation in the natural laws of the universe. Something felt off.

I began to question the foundations.

If it is possible to live without money, what else is possible? What do I really need? What am I capable of? Do I need to search for it, work for it, or is it already within me – was I born with it?

I booked a flight to Lima, Peru and a return flight to Dallas, TX. I had no plans, no cell phone, no tourist adventures, no hostel to sleep in, and no money. Just a ticket there, a ticket home, and a backpack with some clothes, nuts, and a sleeping bag.

Why Peru? I couldn't tell ya – gut instinct.

I decided not to tell anyone about my little adventure except my roommate who would be mailing me my wallet when I returned to the States. I didn't want to worry my parents, and my father's reaction on Christmas, which may be what you are thinking right now, proved my point.

WHAT!? YOU DID WHAT? HAVE YOU LOST YOUR FREAKIN' MIND?!

The following took place between the dates of November 8th and December 21st 2017. It is not a story, rather the unfolding of events. The events and conversations are as accurate as could be recalled using my journal from the trip. Names have been changed for privacy.

In the back you will find a short list of some Spanish words and their definitions. If you're a Spanish speaker, I know some of the sentences are cringe worthy - I was just going with the flow, trying to survive.

I would like to apologize to Ms. Walbert and Señor D, my high school Spanish teachers for treating their classes like study hall. You were right, I should have paid attention in class.

1 LEAP OF FAITH

Day 1 November 8, 2017

This is it. Today's the day, I thought to myself as I lay there in my bed. I looked around at the room that I had become accustomed to waking up in for the last year and a half - the white walls, the painting from my brother, my monstera plant sitting there in the corner. I looked over, my companion still asleep next to me. *Enjoy this. It will soon be gone.*

My mind began running. *Let's go. Get out of bed. Your flight is in a few hours. You still need to pack, get a map, print your boarding pass, and chop your hair...* I reached up grabbing my ponytail. *This has got to go before you get on that plane. Alright, Alright... I'm up.*

In a whirlwind I began packing, waking the sleeping beauty.

"Hey, do you still need to run out and get a map?" she asked, still lying in bed, "I'll take you to Barnes and Noble."

Together, we rushed to the Grove and scoured the Travel section, searching for maps of Peru. *How is this possible? How are there no maps of Peru?* Then, tucked behind an Argentinean map, I found a large map covering the entirety of Peru. *This will do,* I thought to myself.

"What about this? It has a few maps in it," She handed me a travel book on Peru with a few detailed maps of Lima.

"Couldn't hurt. I should be good with these. Let's go," eager to get back and finish my to do list.

"What about a Spanish Dictionary? Do you have one of those?" she asked.

Shit. No. I hadn't even thought about that yet. I don't speak Spanish.

"Uhhh... No... "

"Here. This will probably come in handy." She handed me a pocket sized English/Spanish Dictionary.

Why are girls always so much more prepared? Good thing she rolled with.

"Alright, now were good. Let's cruise. "

Back at the apartment, I laid everything out on the bed in the back room. *Pack light- move swiftly. Pack light- move swiftly.* I reminded myself. I packed few items into an old backpack: a journal, 2 pens, a toothbrush, toothpaste, a few t-shirts, 3 pairs of socks, 3 pairs of boxers, a pair of leggings, a canteen, water purification drops, a long sleeve, a light pullover fleece, a few bags of nuts, a map of Peru, a book on Peru, a dictionary, and my passport.

"Yo dude, here," Adam entered the room holding up a piece of paper.

"Your boarding pass, I printed it for you at work."

"Ahh thanks dawg."

"You all set?"

"Almost. You got the clippers?" I asked, grinning.

"Oh no, no! Are we really gonna do this?"

We had both been growing our hair out since we became roommates over a year and a half ago.

"What, are you scared…Scared to… LET GO?" I joked.

"No, its not…that I'm scared…I don't care…really…it's just…it's just I don't think were gonna have enough time, " he explained.

"Come on, dude. It'll be quick."

"You sure? How quick?.. I just REALLY don't want you to miss your flight," he said, continuing to stall as he brushed his fingers through his locks of hair.

"Dude, I'm fine. I'm not gonna miss my

flight."

"Fine! Fine! Fine. Let's just do it," he agreed, running off to grab the clippers.

30 minutes later, we stood there in the living room, clean cut, with our mains covering the floor.

"Alright, you ready to roll?" he asked.

I thought to myself going over a mental checklist. *Bag is packed. Hair is cut. I have my passport.* The growling of my stomach interrupted me.

"Yeah. Yeah, I'm all set," I rushed into the kitchen and grabbed the Tupperware with last night left over's - Beyond Meat meatballs and homemade tomato sauce. *This is so good, enjoy this enjoy this*, I reminded myself as I dug into the remains.

"Ah this is probably the last time that you're gonna eat real food for a while, huh?" Adam reminded me as I polished off the container.

"Yeah. Probably," I said, grabbing my bag, "Let's Roll."

Before exiting the apartment, I reached into my back pocket and pulled out my wallet.

Don't think, just do it.

I placed it down on the coffee table, and walked out the front door.

Outside the car, I gave her a hug goodbye,

"See you in a bit," I said with a smile.

And the journey began. Still having my phone on me, I called my mother one last time as we drove to LAX. *Do not worry your mother. She is already upset that you are leaving the country without a phone. It will be the longest you haven't spoken to her.*

"Hey, Mamma I'm on my way to the airport, I love you. I'll see you in Dallas."

"Do you have everything you need? Everything? You're sure, you have everything?"

"Yes mom. I have everything I need."

"Promise?"

"Promise."

"What about your sister's address, for when you get back to Dallas?"

"No. No I don't have it."

"Write it down."

I took out my notebook and wrote down "8476 Belmont Ave Dallas Texas." I could hear tears coming from the other end.

"Mother, don't worry. Listen to me, you're gonna blink, you're gonna blink your eyes, and I'm gonna be back and were gonna be in Dallas together, sitting across the table, sharing some poppy seed bread and eggplant, and laughing, and crying, and telling stories. I love you. "

"I love you baby. I love you so much my sweet, sweet angel."

"I gotta go. We're here. I gotta go. I love you."

"I love you."

I hung up, turned off my phone, and handed it to Adam, "Alright man, this is it."

"I'll mail this to Dallas with your wallet so you can have it when you get back."

"Thanks dawg."

"Love you man, travel safe."

"Love you too homie, see you soon."

There I was, standing in line for security, not knowing what was coming next. I felt as if I were standing on the edge of a cliff, about to jump, and praying- praying that the parachute would open on the way down. *Faith. Have Faith.*

On the flight from LA to Mexico City, the flight attendant came around serving a meal, ham and cheese croissants with applesauce. I was faced with a decision that I would face many times throughout this journey. I had come to the conclusion that my survival, my life did not depend upon the killing or harming of other animals, so I would not eat meat.

"Just the applesauce," I said with a smile. I took the small container and packed it in my bag, not knowing where my next meal would come from.

On the second flight from Mexico City to Lima, I was faced with the same decision as the flight attendants came around with dinner. The mind tricks began. *You haven't eaten since those leftovers this morning, and it's almost midnight. You don't know if you're going to get offered food again. Maybe you should get the sandwich.*

"Just the applesauce," I told the woman, my stomach growling as I eyed the dinner of the man next to me.

2 THE FIRST 24

Day 2 November 9th

"Passengers, please return your seats to an upright position and make sure your table trays are put away. All loose items are to be stored in the overhead bins. Prepare for landing in Lima. The current local time is 6:08 AM," came over the intercom. *This is it man. You're here.*

Buckled into my seat, ready for landing, I struck up a conversation with the man sitting next to me. He was a Peruvian native, living in the states, visiting family in Lima.

"Where are you staying tonight?" he asked me.

Wow! That is a great question. Gotta figure that one out still, I thought to myself.

"I don't know. I don't really have any plans," I responded, casually.

"I'll give you a little advice. Go straight to Mira Flores. It's where all the tourists stay. There's clubs, bars, restaurants -it's safe there. There's a place there I usually stay. It's great, only like 30 US dollar per night. Take out a pen and write it down. It' a place called the Hotel Pada Mericado, on the 15th block of Anendale Ave. Just take a cab straight from the airport and drop off your bag at the hotel."

Cabs? Hotels? If only he knew, I thought to myself.

I entertained the man, jotting it in my journal, "Thanks, man."

"My friend," he grabbed my arm and looked at me directly in the eyes, "Please be safe. Lima is a dangerous city. I wouldn't walk anywhere, especially with a bag," he instructed me, nodding down to my backpack on the floor.

Well.. that's some great news..

"Alright man… Thanks.."

I exited the plane, followed the other passengers out of the terminal, into the lobby, and out through the sliding airport doors to the passenger loading zone. A flood of cab drivers immediately bombarded me.

"40 soles, Mira Flores!"

"30 Soles! Mira Flores!"

"25 Soles, Lima! Lima! 25 Soles Lima!"

"Mira Flores! Mira Flores!"

Everyone was speaking Spanish. I couldn't understand a thing. I was in an unfamiliar land, and the conversation with the man from the plane was still fresh in my mind. A wave of emotions came over me as I stood there, staring off at the rows of cabs lining the road. *What's your move? What's your move?*

I retreated back inside and found a place to sit down. I was paralyzed by fear as I sat in that airport lobby. *What's your next move? I don't know. I really don't know.*

I sat glued to that bench, and took out a bag of cashews. I began munching on my rations for the next 6 weeks. I was tired from the flight, and it had been almost 24 hrs since I had eaten the leftovers. *Just a few handfuls, just a few, just a few.* One after another, I placed a cashew in my mouth replaying the conversation in my head. "Lima is dangerous. Take a cab straight from the airport."

Before I knew it a quarter of the zip-lock bag was gone, and I was still hungry, sitting there on a bench in the airport lobby. *You just ate a few days worth of food. These bags have to last us 6 weeks! Cabs, buses, public transportation- these things are no longer options. You have 2 options. You either sit here, and in 30 minutes, you'll still be sitting here and half the food will be gone… or... you start walking.*

I grabbed my bag and exited the airport for the second time. Again, the cab drivers began approaching. I smiled, for this time I had a plan.

"Mi amigo, donde esta Mira Flores?" I asked,

using the little Spanish I knew as I pointed up and down the street.

The man pointed south, "30 Soles, I take you."

"Gracias, Muchas Gracias. Pero yo… caminar, walk," I made a walking motion with my fingers not sure if I was using the right vocabulary.

"Caminar! You walk? Mira Flores?" He laughed.

"Si. Si." I smiled. "Cuantos .. uh…horas?" I asked.

"Eh… seis.. siete.." he responded, clearly amused.

"Y Lima, cuantos horas a Lima?"

"Ehh quatro… Cinco," he replied shrugging his shoulders.

I pointed south… "Lima?" I asked.

"Si. Si. Lima." He laughed.

"Muchas Gracias," I said with a giant grin and began walking south, out of the airport.

I reached the main road, just as the morning rush hour was beginning. It was a warm, foggy morning, and I found myself beginning to sweat as I trekked down the busy highway. Buses and cabs zipped by blasting their horns. I walked down the road, observing as kids rushed with their backpacks off to school. People were loading onto buses, slammed past capacity. Bus stop after bus stop, men hung out the windows of the buses, chanting names in Spanish - towns, streets, I couldn't tell. Stray dogs roamed the streets and the buildings were in desperate need of repair. I found myself on an overpass, standing over a brown, muddy, polluted river. Plastic, clothes, and old rubble from construction littered the banks like a dump, *Hello Lima.*

After about an hour of walking, I spotted a friendly looking couple standing outside a home.

"Mis amigos, Donde Esta Lima, downtown? The road, the road to downtown." I elaborated, hoping they would understand me.

"Lima? El autobus, allí." The man pointed to a bus stop across the street.

"No, no usar autobus, solo caminar," I responded with a smile, again making the walking motion with my fingers.

"Caminas? Downtown? Usar autobus. No caminar. Very far."

"Si. Si. Esta bien. Me gusta caminar. Necessito directions." I explained in my Spanglish.

There was a bit of confusion. The couple debated with each other in Spanish.

"Uhhh.. No se exactamente. But, that way. Colonial Ave." They pointed South- East.

"Gracias."

I walked until I hit Colonial Ave, and continued walking down the street as shops were beginning to open, observing more kids rushing off to school and more women selling pan, snacks, and coca-cola. I had been walking for the better part of the morning. The sun was well overhead, now beating down from above. I could feel the skin on my face starting to burn. *Sunscreen. You didn't pack sunscreen.*

In the distance I could see what appeared to be a town center, a plaza of sorts. I attempted to cross the street but retreated to the curb as a cab zipped past, almost clipping my leg. *Shit, this isn't America.* I stood on the curb and observed. The people would run across the street in packs to avoid being hit by the cabs and buses. *The pedestrian does not have the right of way, noted.*

I reached the plaza, Av. Nicolas De Picola. Curious how long I had been walking, I asked a stranger. "Que Hora Es?"

"Dies y siete."

"Gracias."

Staring off at the beautiful plaza, without a cell phone or camera, I took out my journal and began sketching. As I sat there on the corner of the plaza, 2 teenagers approached me, a gypsy looking couple, "Sir, we are hungry. Do you have any money?"

I smiled, "No, Yo tambien. I don't have any money either."

I could tell they didn't believe me, but they continued walking. I looked around me and noticed that I stuck out like a sore thumb. I continued wandering down to the San Martin Plaza. There was a beautiful statue in the center of the courtyard surrounded by flowers and perfectly manicured, green grass.

As I rested, regaining some energy from the morning trek, I was approached by a boy whose appearance reminded me of Anakin Skywalker from Star Wars. He was wearing a brown poncho and had a buzzed head except for a tail that ran down his shoulder. Speaking zero English, he attempted to sell me some cereal bites.

"Tengo cero soles," I told the kid who was about 18 years old. Instead of walking off like the others before him, he was curious.

"Por que?" He responded with a confused look on his face.

I pulled out my Dictionary and began translating his sentences.

"Porque no tienes? Why don't you have?" He asked in Spanish.

"No necesito. Dinero…uh.. no… es verdad." I responded, giving him my best Spanglish.

"Como vives? How do you live?" he asked.

"No se. Pero…I believe…no necesito."

"Que comes? What do you eat?" he asked.

I pulled out a bag of cashews and gave him a handful. In return he gave me a small pack of cereal bites.

He sat there next to me for the next 15 minutes– trying to make sense of the situation. He was fascinated by the idea of living without money. We talked about a society that could function on resources. He was struggling to make money to support his mother and sister.

"Donde dormir? Where will you sleep tonight?"

"Honestly, no se… como te llama?

"Marco.. you?

"Michael."

"Bien. Necesito ir. Chow Michael, mi hermano." He stood up and gave me a hug. I stood there hugging him back, *my first friend in Peru, mi hermano.*

As he walked off, his question popped back in my head. *Where are you going to sleep tonight?*

I looked around the plaza and spotted a sign on the second floor of a building right off the plaza that read "San Martin Hostel."

Bingo!

I walked up the stairs and found a man with a brown cap and a mustache sitting behind a large wooden desk. *You need a place to sleep. You just need a place to put down your sleeping bag that is sheltered. You don't need a room, and you are willing to work, clean, cook, whatever he needs. Well… here goes nothing.* I put together my best Spanglish and greeted the man.

"Mi amigo, necessito una place to dormir, pero no tengo soles. Quiero trabajar. Yo soy un chef, trabajar en la cocina or limpiar – todos, hacer todos, solo necessito dormir."

A look of absolute confusion came over his face.

"Tu necessita una casa?"

"Si."

"25 Soles."

"No, no, no. No tengo soles. Necessito trabajar for space to put my sleeping bag," I tried explaining.

He called back to a back room and was joined by a teenage boy.

"Tell him," the man said, pointing at the boy.

"I don't have money. I want to work. I just need a place to lay my sleeping bag."

The boy translated it into Spanish for the man behind the desk.

"Ah. No, No. Necesitas Soles. 25 Soles," the man replied.

I pleaded, "Please, I clean, cook, todos, I don't need

a room, just small space to lay my bag."

"No, 25 soles. 25 soles."

This isn't working, just move on.

"Gracias."

I walked out, defeated. *Don't get down. This is just the first stop. You'll find something.* I spent the afternoon, entering one hostel after the next, explaining my situation, and asking if I could work in exchange for a place to lay my sleeping bag.

"35 soles."

"25 soles."

"40 soles."

"Soles! Soles! Soles! Necesitas Soles!"

You need Soles! You need Soles!

"Tengo Cero Soles," I explained as I bartered and pleaded.

One, after another, after another, rejected.

"No, lo siento papi."

"No, necesitas soles."

"No, no lo siento."

After a few hours of repeated rejection, my mind began to race. I found myself, late afternoon, alone in a park in downtown Lima, sitting on a bench, not really knowing what to do next. *Maybe they are right… Maybe you do need soles to live.. maybe this whole thing was a terrible mistake and now you're stuck here on the streets of Lima, homeless. Stop. Stop. No. You know that's not true. You just need to regroup.*

So I sat. I just sat there waiting for the next impulse. I spotted a group of people selling handmade bracelets on a nearby walkway. One of the men had dreadlocks. *Maybe he knows a place.* I walked over and asked the man if he knew any places in or around Lima that offered a place to sleep in exchange for work, or if he knew of any hostels I could try to barter with.

He pointed across the street where he said there were a few hostels for travelers. I approached the first establishment, a yellow building with flags from around the world hanging over the door. I knocked, and explained my situation to the girl who answered. She led me in and called her boss. Hanging up the phone,"35 Soles."

"No, no, you don't understand. Tengo zero, cero. Quiero trabajar para tu. Can I speak with him?"

She called him back. This time telling the man I have no money. She hangs up. "We don't have any more rooms available. You need to leave."

"Gracias, chow!"

I left the hostel, and as I walked out I saw another hostel across the street, except this one didn't have the flags, or the planters flanking the doorway. The sign was yellow and red, faded, and the building was in dire need of a new paint job. *This is a little more my speed.* I put on a smile as I entered to find a girl in her mid 20s folding sheets behind a glass counter in the lobby - a small room with a mini fridge, couch, and counter.

"Hey, I need a place to sleep tonight, but I don't have any soles. I will work, clean, cook, solo necessito dormir."

"No entiendo," she said as she laughed. The girl did not speak any English.

Ok, let's try this again.

I pointed at my sleeping bag and then at the couch. "Yo dormir aqui?"

"Dormir aqui? 20 soles," she responded.

"No tengo."

"No se," she replied shrugging her shoulders, still smiling.

"No, no necesito room. Dormir aqui? The couch?" I repeated pointing at the couch in the lobby.

The girl laughed. "No, no, no. 20 soles."

I began selling myself, "Cocina, la cocina, trabajar en la cocina… solo esta noche un noche."

She continued laughing at me… "Un momento."

She picked up the phone and called someone. *They're talking about me. She's smiling. Yes! She's smiling. This is good. This is good. Maybe this is it.* She stopped smiling, and hung up the phone.

"No, no. Lo siento. But he will be back at 10 tonight," she told me in Spanish.

"Muchas Gracias."

As I exited, I noticed that the sun had begun its descent and the temperature was dropping. I found a seat on a nearby bench, thinking. *I hope it doesn't get any colder than this tonight. It will be dark soon and you don't have anywhere to sleep. Alright man, again you have 2 options. You can keep sitting here feeling sorry for yourself and in an hour you'll still be sitting here… or you can throw more shit against the wall and see what sticks.*

I got up and began wandering down random streets, looking for more signs that read, "Hostel." After being shot down so many times, I began getting used to it. One man was so confused when I told him I didn't have any money that he yielded a large piece of wood, like a bat, and yelled at me to leave. *Could have been the language barrier.* I kept trying, and trying, and trying.

I walked out of a hostel after being rejected, yet again, and thought to myself, *maybe we need to switch up our strategy, maybe try working at a restaurant.*

I turned to my right and saw a building with two signs that read "Vegetarian" and "Yoga."

Bingo! Maybe they need help in the kitchen.

Without hesitation I walked in and greeted the man sitting behind the counter at the restaurant. He was about 40 years old with olive skin and a shaved head except for a small patch near the crown, about 4 inches long. He was wearing a faded, orange robe and sandals.

"Hola, como estás!" I greeted the man.

"Bien, Hare Krishna, Cómo estás?" he replied with a friendly smile.

"Mi amigo, tu necesitas trabajar en la cocina?" I asked, in my broken Spanish, hoping that I was asking the right question.

I continued, "Yo soy un chefe y quiero trabajar in la cocina. Soy Vegetariano."

The man smiled, eyeing me up and down, trying to make sense of the situation.

"Un momento, ven." he signaled me to follow him to the dining room of the establishment.

"Sit. Tell me." He said in broken English.

I began to explain to him that I had a sleeping bag, I didn't have money, I didn't need money, and I didn't want money, just a safe place to sleep. I wanted to work in the kitchen – cooking or cleaning in exchange for a place to sleep.

"Solo tengo un sleeping bag- Necessito dormir esta noche. Quiero trabajar en la cocina – chefe or limpiar, para dormir aqui. No necessito dinero solo dormir aqui. Tengo zero soles."

He was listening. He was intrigued.

"Un momento." He got up from the table and disappeared down a hallway. A few minutes later, he returned accompanied by another man who was sporting the same hairstyle.

"Tell me… Your story," said the second man in English with a thick accent.

I explained my situation.

"Porque? Why you traveling without money?" the man asked.

"Money is not real. Food is real. The sun is real. Energy is Real. But money, money is not natural, it is not true. I do not need it - Dinero no es verdad. Comida es verdad. Sol es verdad. Energía es verdad. Pero dinero, dinero no es natural, no es verdad. No necessito."

He stared at me with a strange look.

"Very good, ven. "

They brought me to a small office in the back of the establishment.

"We have village, yoga community, 2 horas norte. Tiene un programa para voluntarios. You would like to go volunteer?" he asked in his broken English.

I couldn't believe my ears. Was this real?

"Yes! Thank you. Si, Si, Gracias."

"You have food and room to sleep, but you need money, 10 Soles per day."

Damn. I knew it was too good to be true.

"No, No. I don't think you understand. Tengo 0 soles. 0 soles."

He stared at me. I could feel him analyzing to see if I was telling the truth or if I was just crazy.

After a few moments of silence he left the room, leaving me alone.

Maybe there's another option, maybe. Don't lose hope.

The man was in the hallway, on the phone with someone, talking in Spanish at a rate I couldn't comprehend. He returned shortly after.

"It's a OK. I call the village. Tell them your story. Esta Bien. You go."

"Gracias! Gracias! Muchas Gracias!" I was overwhelmed with joy. "When? Tomorrow?" I asked.

"No, esta noche, tonight."

"Perfect. Thank you. Can you give me directions from Google or a map - direcciones?"

"It's a 2 hour bus ride then walk. Here." He handed me a map of the road from the bus stop with directions in Spanish.

"Gracias, but no usar autobus, solo caminar. Tengo 0 soles… Remember?" I asked.

"Ahh. No, no, no caminar!" he responded. "No es possible."

"Si, si es possible! Caminar de la aeropuerto aqui. Solo necesito una mapo y direcciones. Yo caminar!"

"No! No caminar!" he replied insistently and waved me over to his computer where he had Google translator opened.

I read the translated text as he typed, "Lima is very dangerous..

You can be killed…

Traveler was killed….

Organs sold on black market….

No walk…"

Shit. Well you don't have another option. You want food? You want to sleep? You're gonna walk there.

"Its ok. It's ok. I walk. I walk. Just need directions and I'll leave."

"Wait, un momento," the man left me again in

the room. My mind began running with the new information. *Yeah, you don't have anything valuable to take, but they can still kill you and sell your organs. They kill people, man! Stop. You should have never read that. There's nothing to be scared of. You're gonna walk and you're gonna be fine... or they kill you and it won't matter cause you'll be dead.*

A few minutes pass and he returns carrying a helmet and hands it to me. "Grab your bag. Come."

I grabbed my bag and followed him out of the restaurant to a scooter on the sidewalk. "Hop on!" he smiled at me.

I shook my head laughing.

This is too good to be true.

Next thing I know, I'm whizzing through Lima traffic on the back of this scooter, holding onto a Hare Krishna devotee as we weave past busses and cabs. He's punching the sides of busses as we squeeze through traffic. We run up onto sidewalks, zipping by pedestrians, he's still punching cars and busses. We continued cruising through the streets of Lima as the sun was setting.

We pulled off the major road, down a few alleys and arrived at a small bus station. The driver parked the scooter, said a few words to the bus driver, and told me to hop on the bus.

I thanked my new friend for the ride, gave him a hug, and boarded the bus. *Dude, where are you going? It's ok. Just Trust.*

The bus driver greeted me with a smile and a nod as I boarded his vessel, "I will tell you when to get off," he reassured me, sensing my uncertainty.

The bus was slammed. I stuck out like a sore thumb, for this was no tourist bus. I managed to squeeze into a seat near the window, next to a Peruvian man who looked like he had just read his first issue of GQ, wearing slacks, a button down, a tie, and carrying a folder, which listed the different prices of paint, a salesman. The woman across the isle stared down at her phone, scrolling through Facebook posts as she slugged down a bottle of Inca Kola.

As I sat on the bus, exiting the downtown area of Lima, I noticed the extreme poverty outside my window - dirty rivers, destroyed buildings, muddy roads, stray dogs, and a giant billboard of Giselle in her lingerie. I began settling in and resting. The sound of blasting gunshots came over the speakers. The driver had just started the movie for the trip, "The Marine 3 Homefront," an American made shoot-em-up movie about the power of the Marine Corpse. I dozed off to the sound of machine guns firing.

The next thing I knew the bus was stopped. I looked out my window to see farmland and small shelters made of plywood and clay lining the road. The bus driver came back, telling me this was my stop. As I exited the bus, I tried remembering the instructions my friend had given me at the bus stop, "Turn left, and walk straight until you hit the ocean."

The sun had set, and it was beginning to get dark quickly. I started walking down the road, littered with plastic and other pollution, until I reached a fork. The main road continued up and to the left and a small, dirt road continued straight. I stood there looking down the dark, unlit road. *This has to be it. Trust your instincts.*

I started down the dirt road, my mind drifting back to what I had read on Google Translator earlier that afternoon. *They sold a man's organs for money. Can you believe that?* I continued walking down the road, lit by the moonlight. I passed abandoned buildings, dirty streams, patches of desolate land, and cornfields. *Where am I? Is this the right road?*

Dude, you are in Peru somewhere, 2 hours from Lima, on a sketchy road in the middle of nowhere. You have no money, no phone, and no friends. If anything happened to you, you would just disappear. Look. Look around you.

I stood there stagnant, paralyzed by fear, in the middle of the road, looking around me up and down the road.

Why would you do this? Why would you come out here without a phone or map? You don't even know if this village exists. You're trusting some guy with a shaved head and a little patch of hair who barely speaks any English. You're here. You're stuck here. You can't go back. You Idiot.

No. Stop. Stop. Relax. Breathe. You're Fine. You're alive. Just keep walking.

As soon as I managed to calm my mind, I heard a growling noise coming from the darkness up ahead. The growling turned into a vicious bark as a stray dog came running towards me. His bark got louder as he neared. *Shit! Shit! Shit!* He wasn't alone. Out from the brush came 3 others, joining the pack, barking and growling. They got closer and closer. *They can sense your fear. You're a stranger, a fish out of water. Just keep walking. Just keep walking.*

After about 45 minutes of walking, all I could see in the moonlight was farmland and more abandoned dwellings.. *This can't be the right road. Where are you going to sleep tonight?* I eyed the nearby fields, and debated putting my sleeping bag down. My mind began racing again. *You didn't get your shots before you left, and you don't know what animals are out here. Snakes! Rats!... Dude... Relax... Come on. Let's keep walking.*

I continued walking -more farmland, more buildings, then I spotted something on the side of the road... two wooden crosses and names written on a plaque, graves. *Here in the middle of nowhere? How did they die? Stop. Stop. Come on walk.* More growling came from the distance. *Shit. More dogs.* This time I found myself surrounded by a whole pack of dogs, growling and barking, warning me to stay off their territory. *Show no fear. They can sense fear. Show no fear.*

In the distance I saw some light, there was a dome shaped building like the one I had seen on a poster back at the restaurant. *It was real. The village was real.*

I knocked on the side door. No answer.

I knocked again. *I really hope someone is here. I hope this is the right place.*

A few minutes later, the gate cracked open. A guy about my age greeted me, sporting the same hairdo as the other two devotees back in Lima.

"Hello, my friend. We were waiting for you," he welcomed me into the village. *Yes, someone who speaks English.*

He continued to give me a brief tour – showing me the kitchen and the outdoor bathroom facilities. At the village, the human waste was covered with sawdust and saved as "compost" he explained. He walked me back to a grouping of eco-constructed dwellings, opened one of the doors and told me to put my stuff down.

You don't have money so you must give, give, give, and do anything you can to help. Give more than you receive. They are giving you a lot. Make sure you do everything you can.

"Michael, since you are not paying like the other volunteers, there will be more work for you to do. Is that ok?"

"Yes, yes of course."

"This week, you do the compost," He said with a smile.

"Compost? Like the poop?" I asked, wanting to double check.

"Yes. The poop."

Alright man. If this is what you have to do to survive, you're gonna do it. And you're gonna be thankful that you have food and a place to sleep. There is no job too low. You will learn whatever lesson you need to learn, just be happy you're not on the streets of Lima right now.

"Alright cool. Let's do it."

"That's ok with you? The compost?"

"Yeah. It's cool. I just want to help."

"Ok. And Kitchen at 7:30 to help prepare the breakfast."

"Awesome."

"Right now I go to temple for service. You want to join?"

"Yeah. I'm down."

We made our way through the village back to the Temple, a series of "Truly" (dome-shaped) buildings. We removed our shoes and entered to the sounds of beating drums, symbols, and chanting. "Hare Krishna, Hare Krishna, Krishna Krishna, Hare Hare. Hare Rama, Hare Rama, Rama Rama, Hare Hare…."

After the ceremony, the two of us stood under

a pavilion near the entrance of the village as my new friend gave me a summary of the Bhagavad-Gita and the beliefs of the Hare Krishnas. We hung out well into the night, discussing the similarities of different religions and the essence that binds all life together. It was one of those conversations where it feels like your talking for 20 minutes but in reality 2 hours goes by.

I walked back to the room, and rolled out my sleeping bag on the bottom bunk. I laid down, reflecting on the last 24 hours. *What a day. It feels like a dream. ..1 day without money.*

3 GARDEN OF EDEN

Day 3 November 10th

I woke up to the sounds of birds and other animals as the sun's rays poured through the window. I threw my boots on and rushed down to the kitchen. *The sun's up?! What time is it? La cocina at 730. La cocina at 730. Don't be late.* "A wizard is never late - nor is he early, he arrives precisely when he means to." I remembered Gandalf's quote as I rushed down the path. As I arrived, I spotted a clock hanging on the wall outside the kitchen… 7:20. *Perfect.*

Entering the kitchen, I just stood there, trying to take it all in. There was a skinny man, well into his 50s, wearing baggy Peruvian pants, an off white half button shirt with ruffles around the cuffs, and an apron, stirring a large pot over the stove as he whistled. *This man is like a real life Disney character, straight out of Ratatouille or something.* Behind the man, the countertops were covered with crates, upon crates, of fresh fruits and vegetables.

"Hola Amigo, Buen Dias! Hare Krishna!" The man greeted me with a warm smile and a thick Italian accent.

"Hola Amigo, Quiero ayudar, que hace?" I replied, wanting to help.

"Mangos, mangos! Peel and slice," still smiling and stirring the pot, he nodded his head toward a large bowl on the counter, overflowing with perfectly ripe mangos.

I made quick work of the mangos. *Soy un chef.*

"Done."

"Finished? Gracias -

Strawberry! Strawberry!" Again nodding at a crate overflowing with fruit.

There were hundreds and hundreds of strawberries. For the next hour I washed and sliced strawberries. Some were left fresh for the granola, some heated over the stove for a jam, and some thrown in the blender for juice. I was still slicing strawberries, getting through about half the crate,

"Finished. You finished." He interrupted me with his broken English, still smiling. He went outside and rang a bell, calling in all of the inhabitants of the village.

Breakfast was served.

Everyone sat around a table made from a massive slab of wood, enjoying the meal of granola, bananas, strawberries, papaya, mango, and fresh juice.

After the meal, my friend from the previous night greeted me.

"Michael...time for your service."

Compost, you're gonna be working with human feces. Stop. It's not that bad. I prepared myself.

"Today, you work with Antonio," he nodded to a Peruvian kid sitting at the table still finishing his breakfast.

"Compost?" I asked.

"No." He replied chuckling to himself. "No compost. Today, you work with the animals."

"Animals! Bueno." *Thank God. Hare Krishna!*

Equipped with a machete and wheelbarrow, we exited the village gate and walked to a cornfield across the street. We chopped stalks of corn with the machete, piling bundles and bundles of corn, 2 overflowing wheelbarrows worth.

"For el Toro, Bull," Antonio informed me making the symbol for horns with his fingers.

Wheeling the heavy load back through the village, I saw in the distance, the toro, a massive bull, by far the largest cow I had ever laid eyes on. Nearing the fence, I could see that he was not alone, but he shared his pen with a little billy goat. His tail was wagging with joy, as we got closer with his meal. We unloaded one overflowing wheelbarrow into his feeding stall, except for a few stalks, which we gave to the goat.

"Come todo," Antonio explained.

"Todo?" I asked staring at the pounds, and pounds of corn.

"Si. Come mucho."

I stood there amazed, watching as the bull made ears of corn disappear with one bite. Quickly making dispose of the bounty we had fetched for him, he stood there "mooing" and wagging his tail. *What a magnificent creature.*

After feeding the bull and the goat, we walked over to a pasture where 3 horses were grazing.

"Caballos" he explained, as he brought them one by one from the pasture to the stalls to brush. He cautioned me when we got to the third horse.

"Cuidado! Kick!"

This horse was the youngest of the trio and still had a bit of his wild side. I brushed while Antonio went around cleaning the horses' hooves with a pick.

"Bath time! Bath time!"

One by one we took the horses and sprayed them down. The first 2 were easy. Now it was time for the young gun.

Antonio reigned in the horse as I sprayed him down with the water. After his bath, we walked him back to the pasture. He was not happy to be clean and kept shooting us dirty looks. Once we got him tied up again in the pasture, he stared at us, made sure we were looking, then dropped right onto his back, rolling in the dirt as if to say "Ha! I do what I want!" - We both just stood there, drenched from the hose, shaking our heads and laughing.

Next, we shoveled the pens and composted the manure. As we were finishing up, the bell rang.

"Michael! Almuerzo." It was lunchtime.

We made our way back to the kitchen. There on the table was a massive array of fresh fruits, vegetables, rice, and potatoes. I eyed down the spread: lettuce beets, carrots, and cucumbers. *This is amazing. Fresh fruits and veggies straight from the garden, you spoiled, spoiled man. Be thankful, just remember to give more energy than you take.*

After the meal, I made my way to the kitchen to see if help was needed in preparing the dinner. There was an older woman, "Madre" rolling out dough.

"Hola Madre, quiero ayudar," I told her, wanting to help.

"Aqui," she handed me a large bag of peas that had to be peeled.

"You can do outside."

I sat outside at the table and began peeling the peas, one at a time, cracking the pod, peeling it back, and removing the peas. It was very relaxing. *Look at you man, granola and fruit for breakfast, a heaping bowl of veggies for lunch, hanging out with animals all day, this is all pretty perfect…*

"Hello, would you mind if I helped you with that?" a woman's voice with a French accent came from behind me.

I turned to see a beautiful girl with long dark hair standing beside me.

"Of course," I slid over on the bench making room for the beautiful stranger, placing the bag between us.

As we sat peeling peas, I learned all about my new friend, her travels all over Europe and South America, her passion for sustainable apparel, and her dream to start a lingerie brand.

Ding! Ding! Ding!

Is that the dinner bell?

We both looked at each other in shock. I looked around. It was dark out. I hadn't even noticed the time passing. There, in front of us, was a massive bowl of peas all taken out of their pods.

"It can't be dinner. What about the peas?" We laughed.

Dinner that night was a pea-less vegetable soup.

After dinner, my new friend and I made our way to the temple for the evening ceremony. There was chanting, music, and a lesson from the Bhagavad-Gita.

Returning to my room after the day's activities, I walked past a guy in his late 20s, sporting an unkempt beard and a grown out buzz cut, another traveler. He was sitting outside the kitchen, the only location with wi-fi, watching an episode of Dragon Ball Z. *Is he really watching Dragon Ball Z? It can't be. I haven't seen that since elementary school.*

"Dragon Ball Z?" I asked.

"Si! Si!"

His name was Fabio. He was from Brazil, backpacking across South America and was staying in the same building as me, on the second floor. Too tired to stay up chatting, I retired to the room and quickly dozed off.

Day 4 November 11th

I was awoken by the sound of footsteps. I opened my eyes to see Fabio climbing down the ladder, the room still very dark, for the sun hadn't risen.

It can't be time to get up, the suns not even up.

"Fabio, Que hora es?"

"4:30"

"Donde va?"

"Templo…you want come with me?"

Hm… this sleeping bag is pretty warm. It's still dark. You can sleep for 3 more hours. Come on… Don't be soft.

"Yeah, I'm coming."

We walked near the outer fence surrounding the village, cutting through a patch of growing lettuce, past a row of watermelon and other squash- like vegetables, past a giant life sized, statue of a blue Krishna playing his flute, to the entrance of the temple. Pausing to remove my shoes, I entered behind Fabio. As we walked toward the alter in the front, my friend stopped in the middle of the temple, got on his knees, laid flat on his stomach and extended both arms over his head. I bowed my head in reverence. Two others were already deep in worship at the temple, chanting an unfamiliar mantra in the Vedic language to the sound of symbols.

Over the next hour, the 4 of us chanted and played instruments, celebrating life in our own way. After the chanting, my friend Fabio shared a passage from the Bhagavad-Gita in Spanish. The discussion continued as the sun came up, and we ended our ceremony with a closing chant, Hare

Krishna.

After the ceremony, I made my way to the kitchen to join my new friend Raul in preparation for the breakfast.

"Hola Raul! Buen dias, Que Hace?"

"Michael! Michael! Hare Krishna!" he greeted me with a hug.

"Papaya, Papaya!" he instructed, nodding to the counter near the sink where 4 massive papayas, larger than my head, were awaiting to be prepared for the morning feast.

Cutting and peeling the papayas, my mind drifted again. *This place is magical. It's almost too good to be true.*

"Hola, Buen Dias!" I heard a French woman's voice. "I want to help!"

It was Stella.

Over the next hour and a half the three of us whipped up a feast for the village.

After breakfast, I continued working in the kitchen for the remainder of the day, washing and cutting vegetables, helping the chef prepare for the lunch and the dinner. After dinner, Stella and I walked over to the Temple together for the evening service. A larger group of about 10 of us gathered in the temple that night, chanting and singing praises in the Vedic language.

On the walk back from the temple, Stella and I discussed the beliefs of the Hare Krishna's. Although there were some rules and traditions that we couldn't make sense of, we both rather enjoyed the services. I said goodnight. It was getting late, and I knew I had an early morning.

Back in the dwelling, wrapped up in my cozy sleeping bag, I drifted off to sleep...

November 12th - 22nd
Days 5 – 15

My experience at Eco Truly was quite magical. The days were near perfect. It was like living in the Garden of Eden. It was a village bordering the beaches of Pacific Ocean, with fresh food straight from the land, kind people, music, spiritual teachings, and yoga. There were small dome shaped structures built up on the surrounding hills, overlooking the Pacific where I would go to do meditations in the morning, before preparing the breakfast. Some of my biggest takeaways from my time there were the amazing conversations with the other volunteers and the Devotees.

When asked what to do with his life, and how to spend his time, the devotee answered,

"Be like sugar. Give sweetness, only sweetness."

On another occasion, while standing in line for lunch, I was having a conversation with a devotee about society,

"2000 years ago, the slaves were aware that they were slaves. Today, the slaves wear suits and preach of freedom."

Also, during this time, while carrying wheelbarrows full of water to a nearby school, I saw a human skull lying in a dirt driveway, on the side of the road. It was the same road I had walked in on. I had never seen a skull in that environment before. The only human skulls I had seen in the past were in science class or museums, preserved or behind glass, but there it was lying there on the dirt. It made me consider the fragility of this existence. How we all share the same fate and our death is inevitable. It made me reconsider the dangers of the country, but also gave me peace. *Eventually, you're going to die, but you're alive today, right now, so enjoy it.*

While I was there, I caught a stomach bug, a sickness. My body was unable to metabolize all of the food I was eating, it was going right through me and my energy levels began to fluctuate. This is a common occurrence when traveling outside the country. Although the water was filtered, I assumed it was still the source of my illness.

4 PUZZLE

Day 16 November 23rd

I lay there awake on the bottom bunk of the bed, wrapped in my sleeping bag. Thinking, *you've been here for 2 weeks now. It's time to go, time to move on. You're getting too comfortable.*

Time to go!? I have food and shelter here and you just want me to leave? Leave and go where? Go where?

Relax. When you're ready, you will know. It's getting late, run up the hill and meditate before you prepare breakfast.

I hopped out of bed putting on my boots and made my way up the steep sand dune to the Truly, looking out over the ocean.

After helping prepare the meal, I sat at the large table, eyeing my bowl of fruit and granola with extra appreciation, feeling that my time there was coming to an end.

"Hola Michael. How are you doing?" asked

Prabhu sitting a few seats away at the head of the table.

"Good. Good."

"Are you enjoying your time here?"

"Yes. Yes, I am. It is wonderful. Thank you."

"Very good. Are you going to the other village?" (We previously had a conversation about another village in Peru called Kadagaya, which was constructed under the philosophy of a Resource Based Economy.)

"No, Not this trip. I don't think it's going to work out."

"Hm.. would you like to go to Cusco?"

"Cusco?!"

"Yes. We have a farm out there in the Sacred Valley. Maybe you can go work there, if you would like."

"Yeah. That would be awesome. "

"Ok , I will give them a call this afternoon and see."

"Thank you."

     After breakfast, I was assigned to work with Don Guiermo, the head of agriculture at the village. Accompanied by two other volunteers, Alice, a French girl who dreamed of starting her own eco village/bed and breakfast for travelers in France and Lexy, a young girl from Germany. The four of us began weeding a large field of flax seed. As we made our way down the rows, we discussed life at the village. It seemed the village was able to function because at its core, the Hare Krishnas were devoted to service. They were not tempted by the lifestyle of modern civilization, giving them a solid foundation, a community upon which the village was built.

"Is a village like this possible without religion?" asked Alice.

The bell rang, lunchtime.

Finishing my meal, I made my way over to Prabhu's Office where Diego and Prabhu were hanging out on their computers. As I got closer, I could hear the music blaring from the speakers. "Hare Krishna Hare Krishna…"

"Michael! What's up?" asked Diego in his Columbian accent.

"Any word from Cusco?" I asked.

"I will call my friend now, hold on," Prabhu grabbed his phone, lowered the speakers, and left the office.

Returning a few minutes later with a smile across his face,

"Michael, I spoke with Mahakala in Cusco, you're all set to go. I told him you are traveling without money so you don't need to worry."

"Gracias. Muchas Gracias."

"Here. I will write down the address of temple in Cusco and Mahakala's phone number. Here," as he handed me a small piece of paper.

Here it is. The next piece of the puzzle. Cusco.

"You just have to get there," he said with a smile.

"Thanks man. I really appreciate it."

"How are you going to get there?" He asked, still grinning widely.

That, my friend, is a great question. How are you going to get there?

"Not sure, maybe hitch-hike."

"Hitch hike! Have you done it before here in Peru?"

"Nope, not yet. This will be my first time. Have you?"

"No, of course not. It is very dangerous."

"Thanks again for the address," I replied quickly before he could elaborate.

"Of course. I am excited to hear about your journey. When will you be leaving us?"

"Tomorrow morning."

I left the office and went back to the art center to finish the bracelet I was making for my mother. The third bell rang for dinner. Madre had prepared mashed yucca with carrots and olives on top; it was flattened onto a pan and baked. *My favorite.* I enjoyed my last dinner and went to the temple for one last ceremony.

After the program, I laid out the map in my room, formulating a plan for the journey ahead. The distance from Lima to Cusco is 1078 KM (670 miles) through the mountains or 1486km (923 miles) through Arequipa. First, I had to get back to Lima. The highway from Lima I had come in on was visible from the village. It ran along side the edge of a large sand mountain. At night I would look up and see the lights from the truck traffic. I could skip the long walk down the dirt road, and cut straight up to the highway. *You're 2 hours north of Lima by car, maybe a 2 days walk. First thing, get to Lima. Tomorrow morning we hike up to the road, and journey towards Lima. Everyone keeps talking about these 24-hour buses that run straight to Cusco from Lima. You're gonna find one of those once you reach the city.*

I laid there in bed, praying to the essence that had protected me and guided me this far. *Thank you for this bed. Thank you for these walls and this shelter. Although I do not know the next place I will sleep or eat, I trust that you will continue to guide me.*

5 JUMP

Day 17 November 24th

I sat there at the main table, staring down into my bowl, heaping with granola, papaya, strawberries, and bananas. *I am so thankful for this food. I am so thankful for this food. I am so thankful for this food. This is it man. It's about to get real again.*

After breakfast, I packed my bag and walked the grounds, saying goodbye to all of the new friends I had made over the past 2 weeks. It was time to depart.

I walked out that front gate, that same front gate that had offered me shelter and protection. Standing on the other side of the walls, I was back in the wild. I left, walking up the sand dunes leading up to the highway. I climbed the slope, chanting, and smiling. I stood there, halfway up the mountain looking down on the village. It was different. I was not doing it for exercise, or for fun. This time I would not pretend I was an astronaut as I plunged down the sleep slope like a man on the moon, for this time there would be no descent back to the village. *It's time to move on. Trust.*

I summited the mountain, reaching the highway. After a few moments, I saw a truck approaching from the distance, heading south. Butterflies began whirling around my stomach. Without missing a beat, I stretched out my arm and raised my thumb high in the sky. The truck came closer, and closer. I smiled. *This is it.* The driver looked at me. We made eye contact. He glanced back at the road, then back at me, then back at the road. He was getting closer. *Slow down. Slow down. Slow down.* ZOOM… He whizzed right by me.

It's ok. We'll get the next one.

Another truck appeared off in the distance. I raised my arm higher this time, my thumb extended further. *Come on come on….* Zoom! I felt the gust of wind over my entire body as the truck blew right by.

Another truck, carrying corn, with 3 guys sitting in the front cabin came cruising down the road. I made eye contact with the driver. They're getting closer. They're smiling and laughing. They see me. The man in the middle points, 1,2,3… no room shaking his head as they zip past.

Another, then another, then another, each time my arm going higher and my thumb straighter. Zoom! Zip! Whiz! - right by me, standing there with my backpack on the side of highway.

Should we start walking to Lima? Not yet. We're

gonna catch something. Trust.

The next vehicle coming down the road was a blue bus. I stood there on the shoulder of the road, arm stretched, and thumb up. As it got closer it began slowing, slowing. The bus came to a halt on the side of the road about 20 yards in front of me. I sprinted towards the bus as the folding doors opened with a hiss.

I stepped onto the bus.

"Tengo zero soles," I greeted the drivers, wanting there to be no confusion over my intention to hitch a ride. The driver and his associate looked at each other with a look of confusion. I stood there in the entrance of the bus, and repeated myself.

"Tengo zero soles."

They both stared at me for a moment longer. The associate looked at the driver and yelled something to him in Spanish, then waved me in, shaking his head.

"Gracias. Muchas Gracias."

I entered the back cabin, "Donde va?" I asked, finding a seat in the front row.

"Lima," the woman across the isle from me responded.

"Gracias, Gracias," I responded, smiling, absorbing the comfort of the seat and basking in the victory. I sat there gazing out the window, as we sped down the road.

First hitchhike in Peru… check…and everyone was trying to scare you. Look, look how fast we're moving. Every mile, you would be walking this right now. This would take you two days in the hot sun.

We entered the city of Lima, and the bus driver came back to ask my stop.

"I don't know" I replied.

"Where are you going?"

"Cusco." I replied.

"Stay on, last stop in Lima – many buses to Cusco."

We reached the final stop, and I gifted a handful of almonds from my dwindling stash to each of the bus drivers, and hopped of the bus. *Energy for energy.* Around me, small shops lined the streets with bright advertisements for tickets to Arequipa, Ica, Nazca, Iquitos, and Cusco.

Entering the first bus station, "Mi amigo," I greeted the man behind the counter. "I have to get to Cusco. I have no soles. I will clean buses, vacuum, wash windows, scrub tires, anything. I just need a ticket to Cusco."

"Uh.. mi amigo.. no entiendo," the man was extremely confused.

"I, yo, Necesito, Need, to go, ir, a la Cusco. Tengo zero soles. No dinero. Entiendo?"

"Ahh.. Cusco, Cusco! Si! Si! Autobus de Cusco! 85 soles."

Here we go again.

Gracias. I smiled at the man, leaving the first station and heading to the one across the street. One after another, I pleaded with workers and managers in my broken Spanish trying to give anything I could in exchange for a ticket to Cusco.

"No, no papi. Necesitas soles."

"No. No. No, mi amigo, lo siento."

It was anywhere from 225 soles for a luxury cruiser to 60 soles for the cheapest ticket. It made no difference. Zero was still zero. I continued down the street hopping from one station to the next. I kept this up for about 3 hours until I had exhausted all my options. I continued walking up the streets scheming up a new plan.

Here you are, back in Lima, a dwindling supply of nuts, 0 soles, no hostel, and Cusco is about 1098km away, at best. (A 245-hour walk, according to Google maps.) Maybe I can get a job, make the 60 soles in a few days, then quit and go to Cusco.

Boom! Look!

There was a sign in the window of a Chinese restaurant, "Se Necesita Senorita."

I entered, "Hola, yo quiero trabajar. Yo limpiar y cocinar, todos.."

The girl behind the counter of the restaurant chuckled as she went to the back, returning with two others. The three of them stood there, smirking as I continued to barter and explain my situation in broken Spanglish.

"Where are you from?"

"Estados Unidos."

Clearly amused, the man responded, smiling and shaking his head.

"No, No, No, Lo siento."

I tried the same technique at 2 other juice shops down the block, which had similar signs. Once they heard I was from the United States, they thought it was a joke. No dice.

Not knowing what to do next or where to go, I continued to wonder aimlessly around the streets of Lima, finding myself back at the park I had discovered my first day in Peru. The sun had long peaked and was beginning to make its descent for the night. *What do I do next? What else can I try? Where am I going to sleep tonight?* As I walked through that park a voice popped in my head. *Sit, just sit, and relax, right here on this bench.*

As I sat, the sun began disappearing rapidly, and I was quickly reminded where the source of my warmth was coming from. The temperature dropped. I reached in my bag and threw on my Under Armor pull over, the only 'jacket' I had packed for the trip. I sat on the bench, shivering, thinking to myself. *You idiot. Why didn't you bring a jacket? It's so cold!* The argument in my head continued. *How was I supposed to know it was gonna be this cold? I thought it was summer in the southern hemisphere…*

Stop. Stop. Relax. You have everything you need. You're not cold. Remember those cold showers you would take every morning with the breathing exercises? That was cold. Remember jumping in the ocean in the middle of January? That was cold. Wim Hoff would be ashamed. You're no iceman. I laughed to myself.

You're right. You're right. This is nothing. I'm not cold. I'm alive. I'm fine.

As I sat there in stillness, a Peruvian girl joined me on the bench.

"Hola," I greeted her.

What started off as a friendly conversation in broken Spanglish, quickly turned into a deep conversation about our journeys. She was studying to be a nurse, unhappy with her life. She had longed to be an actress, and wanted nothing more than to live in LA. I told her I had taken a few classes for acting and was coming from LA, and she would not find happiness in being an actress if she used it as the source of her joy.

"Act now, with friends, if you enjoy it, you can make your way to LA in no time. The door will open, but don't wait to be happy," something was speaking through me. As we continued conversing, she pulled from her purse "The

Alchemist," and referred to our meeting as one of the "omens" on her journey. She was smiling, bursting with joy, and introduced me to her mother who had come to pick her up. We hugged, I said goodbye, and in that moment I knew our conversation was no mere coincidence. In that moment I was no longer cold, no longer worried about where I would lay my head that night for I knew, I knew... *You are exactly where you need to be.*

I found myself wandering the streets, walking to keep my blood flowing. It seemed any wisdom or joy I had gained from the conversation was fleeting as again my mind began racing with a different tone. *You're cold. You're alone. It's getting late. You need shelter,* it reminded me. I walked past an outdoor mall. I entered, the walls blocking the wind, temporarily relieving my chill. I walked past Cinnabon, Burger King, and a dozen other establishments that made me forget for a moment that I was not back in the States. I wanted to condemn the commercialization, the capitalism that was spreading and infecting these other countries, but I couldn't. It was warm. *How can you condemn this? It is serving you. . It is giving you shelter. It is serving its purpose. Look, look at all the people here, wanting this as a part of their experience. When this place no longer has people giving it energy, it will not last and it will fade away.*

I continued walking the mall, past a stairwell that seemed to be the source of the heat. It was warm. *Thank God, it was warm.* I sat there, leaned against the railing, in the stairwell, with my backpack and sleeping bag. I pulled out the book

Diego had given to me as a gift back at Eco Truly, John Lennon – Search for Liberation, and began reading.

As shoppers walked past, I kept noticing the weird looks and stares I was getting. *Well, I probably look like a homeless man.* Then it clicked. *You are… you are a homeless man.*

The smell of Cinnabon began lofting through the stairwell. *Damn. I'm really hungry. I haven't eaten since the granola this morning.* Reaching into my bag I found the bag of almonds. *Remember, this is your last fuel source, control yourself, just a few. Ok. Ok, fine, 8 just 8 ok?* I counted out 8 almonds and tried to savor each bite. My stomach was craving more.

8?! Come on just a few more. No, no, no. Put them away. Read your book. This is all you have until.. until who knows when. What if Cusco doesn't work out? You still have weeks to survive until your flight home. These are more valuable than you know.

Cool. Good Talk. My stomach was not pleased with my voice of reason.

My body began to get tired. *You can't stay here. They will kick you out at closing.* I left the shelter of the mall, walking out into the streets. I found myself walking towards the hostel from the first day in Lima, the one with the girl that told me to return at 10pm to talk with the boss. As I entered, the girl who I had spoken with before was replaced with a man in his mid 50s. I greeted the man, told him my story, and asked if I could exchange work for a place to lay my sleeping bag.

"No dinero?"

"Si. No dinero."

"Plastica?" He asked pointing to a sign displaying various brands of credit cards.

"No sir. No tengo plastica."

"No, no can stay here. Need plastica, soles."

"Bien, Gracias."

Again, I was roaming the busy streets of downtown Lima, and again, like a homing pigeon, I found myself in a familiar plaza. *If I remember correctly, the vegetarian restaurant was right off this plaza.* A few minutes later I was standing in front of the same restaurant that had been my rescue a few weeks prior. *No harm in asking, just give more than you receive.*

I knocked on the door of the establishment and was greeted by an older man. His appearance reminded me of a real-life Mr. Smee, the sidekick of Captain Hook, with thick white sideburns and small spectacles hanging on the tip of his nose. The two of us hit it off, conversing about life and philosophy for the better part of an hour, before he asked me my business at the temple.

"I am on my way to Cusco, I am looking for a place to lay my sleeping bag tonight."

"Ah. Very well. You must speak with the commander when he is finished with Yoga. Come."

He guided me to the dining room, where I sat, awaiting to plead my case with the commander.

The commander joined me in the dining room where I told him my story.

"Yes, yes, you can sleep here tonight. Grab your bag. Come with me."

He led me past the dining room, down a hallway, and opened the door to what appeared to be a pantry from the outside. It was a small room, more like a closet with a ladder leading up to a second floor. Half a dozen pair of shoes were scattered around the base of the ladder. We climbed the ladder, which led to a hidden loft. Yoga mats and blankets were laid out on the floor of the small room. He cleared a spot for me to place my bag and handed me a yoga mat for padding.

"Thank you. Thank you. Thank you." I felt as if my words were not doing any justice.

"Quiero Ayudar." I told the commander. "What can I do to help?"

The devotees were downstairs preparing the space for a large yoga convention that would be taking place the following day at the temple. I spent the rest of the night helping the devotees clean, arrange tables, and hang art in preparation for the convention.

I climbed the ladder back up to the loft, and lay down on the yoga mat, wrapped in my sleeping bag, safe, sheltered, and warm. *You're not on the streets. Again you have shelter. Gracias.*

6 BENCH WARMER

Day 18 November 25th

One by one, the devotees around me woke up to do their morning services and meditations. Although it was difficult to leave my warm cocoon, I climbed out of my bag and made my way upstairs for a morning meditation.

Back in the loft, one of the devotees I had worked with the night before gifted me a clementine and another small orange fruit for my journey.

"This is prasada," he explained to me, "Food that has been blessed. It has high energy, for your journey."

I packed my sleeping bag and the commander insisted that I stay for breakfast before continuing my journey. I made my way to the back kitchen where a few of the devotees were getting ready to eat the morning meal – pan, bananas, and olives.

My new friend handed me a hot mug filled with a dark, thick, sweet - smelling liquid,

"Special cocoa drink for a special day. Hand ground cocoa beans from Peru. The cocoa has natural energy. We need lots of energy for festival today and you with your journey."

I gripped the mug and took a sip.

Holy shit. This was bomb. So delicious. I had never tasted anything like it.

The rest of the gang joined us in the back kitchen as we sat around the table eating pan and drinking cocoa. I told them I was heading to the temple in Cusco, which caused great excitement and commotion. "Cusco! Cusco!" They each began trying to explain to me a different way to get there and how their way was best. *Wow. Everyone is so excited. And my body, my body feels awesome. Must be the cacao.* I took out my notepad and began scribbling down notes:

"Lima , Ica, Panamericana Sur or Pan-American South – 6 hrs, Nazca, Kamana, Arequipa, Pass the Atocongo Bridge".. *Not sure what this means, but more pieces to the puzzle. Pretty much, the main road leaving Lima is the Pan-American South. You gotta get on the Pan-American South.*

I grabbed my bag and asked the devotee for walking directions to Pan-American south from the temple.

"Walking? Go through Mira Flores. Take Brasil Ave Straight until you hit the ocean. Then left. Once in Mira Flores ask someone for directions to Pan American."

"Gracias."

I left the temple and began my journey down Brasil Ave. A few miles in, the sun reminded me of its warmth. As its rays beat down on me, I could feel my skin burning. Sweat dripped down my back, wetting the back of my shirt, pressed against my backpack. My nose slowly crisping, I covered my face with a bandana and continued my trek.

How far have we walked? How much farther is it to Mira Flores? What time is it?

It doesn't matter. You're alive. You're not there yet, and you have one option either way. Keep walking.

I walked for hours before arriving at a beautiful park, which bordered a cliff, which bordered the ocean. I was in Mira Flores. Flowerbeds lined the walkways and freshly cut, perfectly manicured, green grass covered the landscape. Tired from the journey, I decided to take a short nap under a shaded tree.

The sun began making its descent, and I knew it was getting too late to continue on towards the Pan-American South that night. *Spend the night here in Mira Flores. It will be safer...but where?*

I walked a few blocks and found myself in Kennedy Park, a beautiful space surrounded by shops and restaurants. The park was filled with flowers and trees. Artists, students, and tourists, were hanging out, enjoying the space.

I sat on a bench, awaiting my next impulse, the

hunger growing in my stomach, as I had not eaten since the cocoa fiesta that morning. The day's trek had my body craving fuel. *Check and see if you have more almonds.*

"Hello," It was a girl's voice, distracting me from my hunger.

"Where are you from?"

"United States, what's up?"

"My friends and I are doing a project for our English class. Can we ask you a few questions?"

"Of course." *Look at you,* I thought to myself. *You don't have anything and you can still help.*

A few minutes later another group, then another, all wanting help with their assignment, approached me. *Give. Give. Give, man.*

The students left and I was there, again fighting my stomach's commands to eat the remaining almonds. It began getting desperate. *Either way you have until Cusco before you get more food. Just eat them now so you don't have to think about it anymore. You're gonna have a few days without food anyway. Your brother is going 40 days with no food. You'll be fine.* As I finished the thought, I noticed that the bag of almonds was already open in my hands, and I was holding the remains in my palm. One by one, I popped them in my mouth.

Gone. My stomach temporarily satisfied, my attention switched back to my surroundings. The wind picked up and I could feel the rapid drop in temperature. Time to move.

I began exploring the streets of Mira Flores. I found myself again on the coast, however, this time, I was in the midst of an outdoor promenade filled with luxury shops and restaurants. My body was chilled as strong winds were blowing in from the ocean.

As I walked past the shops looking for a restroom, I spaced out for a few moments. Coming back I found myself paused in front of the "Patagonia" store. I was just standing there, staring down the bright blue, puffy, down jacket the mannequin was sporting in the front window. *So warm, so puffy… warm... I want to be warm…* I caught myself. *Come on… keep walking. You're fine, you don't need that.* After using the restroom, and spending 3 cycles in front of the hand dryer, I cruised back past the shops. This time, a different shop caught my eye. A massive picture of Machu Picchu hung behind the counter of a grand wooden countertop. "Luxury Liner to Cusco" the sign read. *Imagine that – soft, leather seats- a place to sleep, meals, and a direct ride straight to Cusco.* As I stood there fantasizing, two girls walked past me to the counter to purchase tickets, both of them wearing matching Patagonia, down jackets, like I had just fantasized about. *Enough! Lets go. You don't want that either… even if you did have money.*

I continued walking the plaza. There was one thing weighing massively on my mind. *You have nowhere to sleep tonight. This might be it. This might be your first night without shelter. For so long I have been trying to avoid this, spending my days bartering for shelter. It's time to face your fear.*

I made my way upstairs to a plaza where some guys were playing SKATE. My attention was drawn to a giant map of Mira Flores in front of a bike rental shop. As I scoured the map looking for a route to the Pan-American South, I was interrupted.

"Are you taking the bike tour?" asked a man with an English accent. Between his appearance and his voice, I was reminded of Pippen, the hobbit in LOTR.

We struck up a conversation, sharing our journeys. He was a vegetarian who had also just quit his job and was traveling until the next wave hit him.

It was good to have company to keep my mind off the cold, my growling stomach, and my sleeping situation. He was shocked that I had made it this long without money.

"Where have you been sleeping?" He asked.

"Well up until this point I have been blessed with shelter at village north of Lima and last night at the temple downtown."

"What about tonight?"

Tonight… tonight…

"Honestly, I have been scared to be homeless up until this point. I have spent so much energy looking for shelter. I think I am finally ready to face my fear and be homeless. Tonight, I will probably sleep on a bench."

We hung out around Mira Flores until around 9 when my new friend returned to his hostel and I entered a mall near Kennedy Park to stay warm until closing.

As they were closing up, I made my way to the restroom and put on all of the clothes I had- leggings, jeans, a wife beater, 3 t-shirts, a long sleeve, and my pullover. All layered up, I walked out of the mall, shelter-less. I began my hunt for a place to sleep. As I walked the streets my mind began running. *You know those guys you would pass on the streets of NY wrapped in their blankets, laying on the sidewalk? You would walk right past them feeling pity, thinking 'How did they end up like this?' Tonight. That is going to be you.*

I walked the streets, delaying my inevitable fate. Starting to get tired, I sat down on a random bench in Mira Flores. There was some lighting from nearby street lamps, a gas station across the street, and a descent amount of foot traffic. After a few moments of sitting, all of the fears and worries about the dangers of Lima began rushing through my mind. *"Lima is a dangerous city"… "They killed a guy and sold his organs."… "I wouldn't walk around with a bag."* I reached in my bag, grabbed my passport, and shoved it down my pants. *This is all you need. If you doze off and they take your bag, you can still get home. On that note, try not to doze off. Just stay awake until sunrise and sleep at the park underneath the tree tomorrow. It will be safer.*

After about 2 hours sitting and shivering on that bench, a security guard greeted me.

"Hey, where are you sleeping tonight?" he asked. He had passed a few times and apparently I was giving off the vibe that I wasn't leaving anytime soon.

"I don't know," I replied honestly, with a smile.

"Where's your hotel?"

"I don't have one."

He shot me a look of confusion.

"What do you mean? What's your plan?" He asked, trying to make sense of the situation.

"I don't know, honestly, I'm just sitting."

He looked very, very confused.

"What about tomorrow?"

"Cusco," I replied still grinning.

Either satisfied with the answer or accepting the fact that he could not make sense of this gringo, he smiled, shook his head, and continued his patrol.

I sat there, alone, cold, finding stillness on the bench. As I sat, a man sporting a black-leather jacket, glasses, blue jeans, and dress shoes sat on the bench opposite of me facing my direction.

"Hola Amigo," I greeted the stranger.

"Hola, De donde eres, Where you from?" He asked in a thick Spanish accent.

"I am from United States. And you?"

"Peru. Iquitos."

"Ah bueno," I replied with a smile. I recognized the name from my map and the signs at the bus station.

He began asking me questions in Spanish, which I didn't fully understand. Wanting to continue the conversation. He got up, pulled out his phone, sat next to me, and we used Google translate to communicate.

He typed, "What do you do for work?"

"In United States I worked at a plant shop, but not anymore."

"Plants?"

"Yes. Making art with plants, succulents, cacti."

"Ok. I am politician."

I nodded. And smiled.

"I am important congressman. I represent Iquitos."

"Cool." I typed still smiling.

"In Peru, politician important and have lot of power. I buy house in Miami."

I smiled and nodded.

"Do you like motorcycle?" he asked.

"Yeah, I had one a few years ago."

"Look" – he showed me pictures of his motorcycles – Harleys – sport bikes.

A small part of me wanted to play his games, to "ooh" and "aah" at his shiny toys, to brag about the partying I did in Miami, the frat president, the motorcycle, the clubs, girls, things. All things I was chasing at that time in my life… It won't bring you happiness. Those things are just things.

I nodded and shrugged.

"You do not like?"

"Things are things," I typed. "No importante," I added.

I could sense a wave of relief come over him, as I was not impressed with his boasting or material possessions.

"What about money? Money is important, and power, popularity?" he questioned.

"No, popularity and money are not real. They are ideas that we choose to believe in."

"What is real?" the man asked.

I sat there, finding stillness.

"Love, energy" I typed. "Amor," I added, feeling as if yet again something else was using me to communicate, as these were not my words.

The man's eyes began to tear and the mood shifted.

"I spent whole life wanting to be politician. I want money, popularity. But I am not happy. "

I just smiled at him, this time feeling sorry, compassion.

"What is your philosophy?" he typed.

"All you need is love. Love more."

"I just want happiness."

"Love," I typed. Smiling.

The man began smiling.

"I have not told anyone else these things. Thank you."

I stood up and hugged the stranger before he walked away, down the sidewalk. It was a conversation neither of us would forget. In that moment, alone on the bench, I felt reassured. *You are exactly where you need to be, sharing what you need to share.*

As I sat there, huddled on my bench, too cold to fall asleep, the security guard returned. I prepared myself to leave as he approached.

"Where is your jacket?" he asked me.

"No tengo," I told the man.

He shook his head. Looking at me as if I was out of my mind.

"Que es?" he asked, pointing down to the sleeping bag strapped to my backpack.

"Es mi sleeping bag." He looked at me and nodded his head, as if to say, "It's ok. You can stay here. Stay warm."

I unpacked my sleeping bag and wrapped it over my shoulders.

"Your backpack. It will get stolen," he added. He pointed to the rope that I used for my sleeping bag.

I grabbed the rope and tied my backpack to my ankle.

"Gracias"

The man stood there smiling, nodded one last time, and walked away.

Sitting on the bench, half wrapped in the sleeping bag, I dozed off…

"Yo, Dude! Dude!" I heard a voice waking me from my sleep and felt someone tapping on my shoulder. In a daze, I opened my eyes to see two American looking guys huddled around me.

"Yo man, are you sleeping here?" the one

asked in disbelief.

"Yeah.. uh.. I am… well.. I was…. What's up?" I replied. My brain was in a hazy, sleep deprived state.

"What! Why?"

I sat there exhausted, staring at the two, wanting to go back to sleep.

"Where's your hostel?" the one asked.

"I don't have one."

"So you're just gonna sleep here on this bench."

"Yeah."

"You're not scared someone's gonna hurt you or rob you or something?"

"I've got nothing to lose."

"How did you end up here?"

"I bought a roundtrip ticket and didn't bring my phone or wallet."

"You didn't bring any money? Not a single dollar?"

"No."

"You're crazy. Damn, that's crazy."

"Dude, well you're not sleeping here anymore

tonight. Come back to our hostel, you can at least put your bag on the floor where it will be warm."

"No, it's alright guys, thanks, I'm chillin' here."

I had finally accepted my homelessness, no longer feeling the need for shelter and protection.

The one grabbed my sleeping bag, clearly having a few drinks in him, "Come on man, I'll carry it, just walk back with us, it's only a few blocks. I can't leave you like this.

"Alright, Alright," not knowing what time it was. *A few hours of sheltered rest couldn't hurt.*

The walk back was entertaining as they had just wrapped up a solid night of partying. Their names were Bryce and Colby, two bros traveling South America together, from Vancouver. We swapped stories and talked about life. They were my new amigos.

7 MAGNETIC PULL

Day 19 November 26th

    I woke up on the floor of the hostel, making sense of my surroundings – I remembered the night before – the bench, the dudes from Vancouver. I got up and quietly rolled my bag. *You've got a long journey ahead of you today. Pan-American South,* I reminded myself. Colby was awake and Bryce was still out cold from the night before. I thanked my new friend and said goodbye.

    As I made my way through the lobby of the hostel, a woman offered me breakfast - bread, jelly, and bananas. I snagged two bananas and some bread and made my way across the street to a park.

    I sat, enjoying my breakfast, feeling thankful for the food, for the energy. As I sat, a mother approached and asked if I could take pictures of her and her son.

    "Of course." *Anything I can do to share my*

energy.

"Full nights rest and food in my stomach, beyond blessed" I scribbled in my journal. *Let's move. Pan-American South today.*

Exiting the park, I asked the first person I saw, a businessman wearing a suit,

"Donde Pan-American South?"

There was a long pause as he looked around, gaining his sense of direction.

"El autobus. 2 blocks. That way." He pointed across the street.

"No usar autobus. Solo caminar. Solo necessito the direction, direcciones?"

"Caminar? Tu? Caminar?"

"Si."

He smiled and shook his head. "Go to corner turn right. Walk straight. Eventually. You will reach Panamericana."

"Muchas Gracias," I thanked the man and started walking.

A few minutes into the walk, I felt the sun beating down overhead, my shirt sticking to my back. *Man, It's hot out. Well it's no longer nighttime and you're still wearing 6 shirts and leggings under your jeans. Ah, you're right.* I stopped right there on the sidewalk, in front of a business building and stripped down to my boxers to remove the layers from the night before. I continued my trek with a t-shirt and jeans- covering my face with a bandana. I walked, and I walked, and I walked.

Before I knew it, I was standing on an overpass, staring down at a massive valley of speeding trucks, cars, and buses, 5 lanes in each direction - the Pan-American South. The trucks whizzed by down below. *The Valley of the Shadow of Death,* I thought to myself. I spotted a bus, one of the luxury busses that took people on the 24-hour direct route to Cusco. *I gotta get on one of those.*

I stood there, staring down. *Well, well, here you are. You've been staring down there for about 15 minutes now, and it seems to me like we have 2 options. You can either stand here watching the trucks go by or you can go down there and put your thumb up.*

I made my way down, under the busy overpass where cab drivers, local busses, and mini-vans, were pulling in and darting off. Women lined the narrow sidewalk selling sweet breads, sandwiches, fruits, and Inca Kola. *This is mayhem.*

Walking a few hundred feet up the highway to an exit ramp to separate myself from those hailing cabs, I raised my arm and put my thumb up. For 20 minutes, cars, trucks, and busses whizzed right by me.

Damn. These trucks are much larger when you're standing right next to them, and they're going fast, real fast. This probably isn't the safest thing you've ever done.

Do you have any other ideas?

No.

All right then, keep your thumb up.

A car pulled off to the shoulder in front of me. I approached the window.

"Where are you going?" asked the driver.

"Cusco," I confidently replied. (Little did I know, this was like standing on a highway near NYC telling someone you're going to Jacksonville, FL)

The man laughed, shaking his head.

"There is a bus terminal down the road, I'll take you there."

"Gracias, but no usar autobus, no usar dinero, only hitchhike." I explained to the man.

"You're going to get killed out here. At least go back to the underpass. You are crazy. Hop in."

As I stood there debating, 18-wheelers continued to zip right by us, a few feet away. I hopped in and he drove me back under the overpass.

One by one, I went around asking the local cab drivers and bus drivers the best route to Cusco. All of them instructing me to go to the bus terminal two miles down the road. One of them offered to take me for free. I agreed and hopped on the man's mini bus for the short ride down to the bus terminal.

I entered the terminal, scanning for signs to Cusco.

200 Soles… 125 Soles..80 Soles.. 50 Soles. *Bingo. Everyone has been leading you here. This must be the next step. You don't have any other options. Give it everything you've got.*

I greeted the two girls behind the counter selling the budget tickets to Cusco and began my bartering.

"First, no tengo soles, no tengo dinero, pero necesito un boleto, a ticket, to Cusco." The girls looked at me confused. "Solo tengo me mochila y"… I unloaded my clothes, Spanish dictionary, and the clementine all on the counter. "I will trade for ticket to Cusco." The girls went through my stuff, laughed, and called in another employee. I asked the new guy if I could clean the bus in exchange for a ticket.

Nope, no cigar.

"Soles, plastica, necesitas," they told me.

I sat on a chair at the bus station, hungry from the days trek, feeling like I had hit a wall in my journey, reflecting. *50 soles… that's like 15 bucks... Think of all those times you've wasted 15 bucks… that's like 1 drink at the Bungalow. 1 drink would get you to Cusco. Dude. Come on man, you don't need soles. You don't need a bus. You were gonna hitch…remember?*

In the middle of the terminal, next to where I

was seated, a man had a booth where he was selling cardboard boxes and wrapping luggage. We began chatting. He was excited that I was from the States, and he wanted to learn English. I gave him my dictionary and in return he gave me a piece of cardboard. I borrowed his sharpie and wrote in call caps "CUSCO."

I took my sign and walked back out to the Pan-American South. I stood there, about 40 yards from the bus station with my new sign, hoping to catch a big fish, one of those luxury buses going straight to Cusco. As I held up my sign, watching the trucks and cars zip by, a few people slowed down to honk their horns and point back at the bus terminal. I could see a few people shaking their heads and laughing as they passed by. It must have been an amusing site to be on the other side. A gringo, standing out in front of a bus terminal, holding up a cardboard sign on the side of the highway, and the destination was over 900 miles away.

I had spent the entire day trekking, bartering, and waving down trucks on the side of the highway. My energy was drained. I stayed on the side of the road as the rays of sunlight were quickly diminishing. There was no other option. The cold wind started to blow through my pullover. *It's cold. It's getting colder. No one's stopping. I'm tired. I'm really, tired. Sleep. I would love to sleep.* I looked around me. I saw highway, a few buildings behind me covered in graffiti, and a few stray dogs wondering around. No park benches to rest on. No security guards. Then, across the highway, I spotted what appeared to be a shopping mall, shelter.

Exhausted and worn down, I made my way across the overpass to the mall. I had low energy, almost in a zombie state as I rode the escalator up to the 4th floor. A couple was playing chess on a life sized bored, and I found a bench nearby.

I sat down, staring off, fighting to keep my eyes open. I wanted to give up. I wanted to cry. I wanted to sleep. I wanted to go home. *Don't fall asleep.* My eyes kept batting shut, my head nodding. *Fight it. Please, don't fall asleep. Please, Please I beg you don't fall asleep. If you fall asleep they will kick you out, and you will be out in the cold again. I've trekked for miles and miles in the hot sun. Just give me some food please. I'm so tired, I'm so hungry.*

I don't know where to go or what to do.

Why did you do this? Huh? Why did you do this! What were you thinking! What were you thinking? We're stuck here in this foreign country, alone with no place to sleep! Nothing to eat!

Stop. Stop.

I sat there. Alone. Holding back tears. I was down. Mentally. Physically. I just wanted to go home. I just wanted to lay down somewhere warm. I just wanted some crackers, anything to eat.

Relax. Breathe. You knew there would be times like this. Just relax. You're alive, right? You had bananas this morning, you're not gonna die, right? Let's go for a walk.

I left my bench and began walking the mall, observing the people, the shops. On my left, a Star Wars exhibit with giant action figures from the original series caught my eye. I wandered around the exhibit, thankful to be distracted from my situation for a few moments. I spotted a janitors closet next to one of the exhibits. *Maybe we can sleep in there. It's dark. Maybe no one will come in.* I fantasized; *you could unroll your sleeping bag. It would be warm…*

"The mall will be closing in 10 minutes," a voice came over the intercom speakers. It was 10PM and my time in shelter was coming to an end. I dug around in my bag and found a small container of applesauce from my flight to Mexico City. I sat on a bench outside the exhibit, staring at the small plastic container. *I'm so hungry…so hungry… Stop. Your brother is in the middle of a 40 day fast right now. He hasn't eaten in 20 days and look at you with this applesauce. You are a lucky, lucky man. Enjoy it.* I sat there on the bench licking the container, savoring every drop of the yellow mash.

On autopilot, too tired to think anymore, I watched as my body carried me back across the overpass down to the Pan-American South where the local buses and taxis were exchanging passengers. As I walked down the road, a man ran up to me yelling with excitement, "Cañete! Cañete! Cañete!" *That sounds kind of funny*, I thought to my self. "Cañete!" I yelled back at the man, laughing.

Smiling, he chanted a bit louder, "Cañete!"

"Cañete! Cañete!" I chanted back.

We both laughed.

"You go to Cañete?" he asked. He was a local driver, and I knew his van ran on soles.

"I don't have any money, but I'll ride with you if you want some company." I said jokingly.

He laughed and continued pacing up and down the sidewalk yelling "Cañete, Cañete, Cañete!" as he herded passengers into the back of his mini-van.

I stood there for a few minutes, observing the scene, passengers hopping from one van to another, over to a bus, then back to a van. I was learning. The van wouldn't leave until it was full so people would sit and wait, get tired of waiting and switch busses. Then the driver would have to start all over again.

"Cañete, Cañete, Cañete!" He was back.

"Cañete, Cañete, Cañete!" I mimicked his chant. "I come with you?" I asked.

He laughed, hesitated and said, "Ok, but when it fills, you hop out."

"Gracias! Muchas, Muchas, gracias!"

I entered the half-full minivan, sitting, partially sheltered, thankful to be out of the wind. After about 20 minutes, the anxious passengers began to abandon ship as the driver continued his chant up and down the sidewalk.

First one, then two, then a third and a forth hopped out the open door. The remaining passengers looked at me to see if I was bailing or going down with the ship. They didn't know I only had one option. Five more minutes passed and the last group hopped off, leaving me alone in the van.

The driver returned a few minutes later to an empty bus, except for the one guy that was riding for free. He shook his head in disappointment; another driver came over saw the empty bus and began laughing at him. Together they continued their song, recruiting people to take to Cañete. It only took them a few minutes to get 8 people in the van.

Finally, the door was shut, and we started to pull out onto the road. There was a lot of commotion. The driver began yelling on the phone in Spanish, and then made a quick right. Immediately, lights began flashing behind us, Policia.

Next thing I knew we were speeding down the road. A right on a small side street, a left through an alley, over a curb - we were running from the cops. I looked around the van, everyone seemed anxious- a bit tense, in disbelief to what was unfolding. It was exhilarating.

The flashing lights no longer behind us, the driver looped back around to the main highway and pulled under the overpass where I had originally boarded the vessel. A man was there, waving his arm, and he began jogging along side the van. The driver slowed for a brief moment, long enough for the man to open the door and get the majority of his body in. A fellow passenger held on to the man, pulling him in as the driver sped off with the door still open. The door closed as we began zipping down the Pan-American South. The driver's friend looked back out the window, and the two began to celebrate their small victory. No policia, no ticket, all-on board, en route to Cañete.

Dude, so what just happened? Where are we going? Where is Cañete?

It looks like were going south. It's the right direction. We just have to keep going south.

As the adrenaline began wearing off, and the bus began getting warmer, I could feel my body enjoying the shelter, wanting to shut down and rest. *You can't sleep, not yet. You don't know where Cañete is and you have to stay on the major road to catch your next ride,* I told myself.

After about an hour or so, the driver pulled off to the shoulder of the road. Another mini van pulled behind him. I looked out the window. *We are in the middle of nowhere. There are no lights from buildings, cities, nothing. Where are we? Why are we stopped?*

The driver turned around and looked at me.

"Cañete?" He asked

"Si."

"Other bus."

I hopped off, a bit confused and loaded the other van. Again, my body quickly began shutting down as it adjusted to the warmth. I kept nodding off, fighting the urge to sleep. *Stay awake. Stay awake.* It was no use since my body hadn't slept since the floor in Mira Flores. It overruled me.

8 CAÑETE

November 27th Day 20 Part 1

I woke to the feeling of a strong nudge on my shoulder. I opened my eyes to the bus driver shoving me, "Cañete. Cañete. Off. Off. Last stop. Off, " he instructed.

Shit. You fell asleep. You gotta get back to the main road.

"No. No, Pan-American south," I said to the driver, my mind in a haze.

"No, off. Last stop."

I wasn't listening.

"Are you going back to Lima tonight? Can you drop me on the main road? Pan-American south?"

"No Entiendo. Last stop. Off," He said sternly, not wanting to play games at this hour in the morning.

I exited the bus to find myself in a small, poor,

farming town. It was somewhere between 1 and 2:30 AM. Stray dogs and a few cab drivers lined the town's main intersection where there was a single street light and a small bus terminal. I noticed I was getting stared down by some of the locals. *You stick out like a sore thumb. This is no tourist town. You're in the heart of it. Do not let yourself fall asleep here. Stay awake until the sun comes up.*

I walked across the street over to the bus terminal. It was well lit and appeared to be the safest place in the town. A bus pulled up to the stop. On the front left windshield was a sign that read, "Ica." I told the man behind the counter my story, asking if I could board the bus for it was nearly empty.

"Necesitas soles."

I bartered and pleaded with the man for a few minutes, clearly he could see I was a fish out of water, but he was not having it. He became stern, growing impatient with my persistence and walked over to the bus driver, instructing him to not let me board the vessel, no matter what.

An elderly woman, about 70, sat outside the terminal selling jell-o topped with whipped cream. Noticing the commotion, she asked me what was going on.

I told her I was trying to get to Ica, on my way to Nazca. I had fallen asleep on the ride here, to Cañete, and now I need to get to the Pan-American South to continue my journey.

"Pan-American South?" she asked gazing up at me.

I stood there staring into her eyes. *There is something mystical, magical, and slightly eerie about this woman. She reminds me of a fortuneteller.*

"Yes."

She pointed down an unlit road that led to darkness. "That way," she said to me with a smile, still looking me directly in the eyes.

"Gracias," I replied, and started walking.

Before we do this, just use your head for one minute. You are about to walk down this road leading into absolute darkness because some woman who reminded you of a mystical fortuneteller told you to?

Do you have another option?

... Didn't think so.

Maybe it's close; maybe you weren't sleeping for that long.

I started off down the road. I walked, and I walked, and I walked, and I walked, and I walked, one step at a time. I walked past fields and small clay buildings most of them marked with graffiti. Rustling and animal noises came from the darkness as I walked by more fields. Then came the stray dogs. I began spotting graves, marked with crosses and tombstones. Sometimes there would be one, sometimes multiple in the same location. *Why are there so many graves on this road?*

Every 20 minutes or so, a car would come down the road. I would try to hitch, doing my best to get the driver's attention to catch a ride out to the highway.

It feels like we've been walking for hours, I'm getting tired, really tired. Can we just lay the sleeping bag down in one of these fields? Please? My body pleaded. *No, come on. We're fine. Just keep walking until the sun comes up,* I told myself as I continued, *one step at a time, one step at a time.*

I was on a dark road in a foreign country, with no phone, no money, no food, alone. I didn't know where I was, or where I was going. I just stood there, stopped in the middle of the road, nobody in sight, and I looked up. I gazed up at the stars, at the bright stars, shining down upon me. Orion was lighting up the sky so brilliantly. I was overcome with this feeling, this unexplainable feeling of absolute peace and overwhelming joy. *You're alive. You're really alive.*

I continued walking. Although it was still pitch dark, I began to hear the calls of roosters as they awoke. *Almost sunrise, almost.* I continued down the road, my body's cravings for sleep and fuel getting so loud I could no longer ignore it.

In the distance, I spotted a man standing under a lone streetlight, waiting on the side of the road. Without thinking, I approached the stranger,

"Mi amigo, necessito dormir – I need to sleep, can I sleep on the floor of tu casa, your house?" I asked, pointing at my sleeping bag.

The man was amused, he understood my broken Spanglish.

"No vive aqui – Trabajar – work. Pero, un familia allí," he replied.

He spoke in rapid Spanish, but I managed to make out a few words. He pointed up the street to a white farmhouse.

"Nice family, ask them, sleep, dormir," he explained still pointing up the road.

"Dormir ayer?" I asked trying to clarify, pointing to the white house.

The man nodded his head and shrugged his shoulders. I looked down the road spotting a white house among the cornfields.

"Gracias".

I continued down the road reaching a large gate and a cement wall which blocked the entrance to the farm. There was a small valley with a stream separating the road from the property, like a moat protects a castle. Without hesitation, I climbed down the bank, around the gate, and up onto the driveway. I made my way onto the strangers land, walking down the driveway toward the house. *Here you are, entering a stranger's ranch, somewhere near a town called Cañete, which is somewhere in Peru. What are you doing? Are you crazy? Have you lost your mind? Yes, yes, maybe I have.* Something in me felt confident, and reassured, like it was destiny. There was a large white house to my right about 3 bedrooms at least. There was another small building across the driveway, resembling a guesthouse of sorts. The night was still dark- I could see cornfields stretching out into the distance. There was a loud, incessant "mooing" of cows. *This is a nice farm. There are a lot of animals here. I feel safe. Maybe you can stay here for a bit and work on the farm.*

I neared the house, staring at the back door. *You don't want to wake or frighten anyone at this hour in the morning. Just sit.* I sat there on the back porch of the house, unpacked my sleeping bag, wrapped it around my shoulders and lay back with my legs dangling off the side. Laying there, staring up at the stars, my body quickly shut down.

I felt a strong pat on my shoulder. *Open your eyes. No. Stop. Leave me alone. I'm tired. I just want to sleep.* I thought. I felt another, stronger pat. I opened my eyes to find a Peruvian man standing over me with a very confused look on his face.

"Gringo. Gringo," he said lightly, waking me up.

"Hola, are you the owner the boss?"

"Que?"

"Tu es un chief? Boss? Farmer?"

"No entiendo," the man shook his head, laughing.

He reached down, grabbed a pebble, and threw it at one of the second floor windows of the house.

A man peaked his head out.

"Gringo! Gringo!" the man called up to the other as he pointed down at me.

The two of them spoke in rapid Spanish. I couldn't understand a thing.

Turning back to me he said "A la ocho or nueve.. 8 or 9."

"I can talk to him at 8?"

"No entiendo."

He walked off into the cornfields, and I immediately passed back out on the porch.

Again, I felt a tapping on my shoulder and awoke to see a man standing over me. He was in his late 40s, wearing blue jeans, cowboy boots, a navy v-neck tucked into his jeans and a beige cowboy hat. He stood there, staring down with a look of absolute bewilderment. He was clean cut, appearing very affluent, and stood with authority. *The boss man,* I thought to myself.

"Hola amigo," I said as I gathered every bit of energy I had to appear up beat and alive. He began speaking to me in Spanish at a rate I could not comprehend.

"No entiendo, solo hablo un poco," I told the man.

"De donde?"

"Estados Unidos."

"Estados Unidos? Tu?" he asked, taken back by my response.

"Si. Visitar Peru."

"Ah…Estados Unidos…. Cuanto tiempo in Peru, how long here?"

"En total, 6 semanas. Aqui por 3 y tengo 3 mas."

"Tienes Passport?" wanting to believe my story.

"Si. Si." I grabbed the passport from my bag.

"Donde en Estados Unidos?"

"LA."

"Y ..how tu esta aqui? How you get here? At my farm?" The man spoke in broken English.

"Yo hitchhike from Lima to Cañete. Y caminar from Cañete.. aqui."

"Caminar? Tu? Camina de Cañete aqui?" he questioned in disbelief, shocked, but amused.

"Si. Si."

He started laughing and shaking his head.

"Very far walk."

"Si. Si," I replied also laughing at the

ridiculousness.

"Porque tu esta aqui? Why? Here in Peru?"

"Es loco, pero, es un experimente. Yo vive con 0 dollars. Compro un botillo, a ticket a LA y Lima y Lima y Dallas. Pero. No bring dinero, money, soles, nunca."

"Nada? Aqui por tres semanas con 0 dinero?" he asked in disbelief that I had survived for the past three weeks with no money.

"Si, si. Trabajar a la finca norte de Lima," I explained.

"Ahh.." he smiled, intrigued. "No usar no dinero? No money?"

"No necessito. Dinero no es verdad. Solo necessito dormir y comida, un poco comida," I told the man.

"Interesante...Que come?"

"La finca. Come a la finca."

"Ahh," the man nodded his head, trying to make sense of it.

I sat there eying the farm. *You're trying to travel hundreds of miles to work on a farm. Why don't you just work here? Maybe this is where it was leading you. Don't get too attached to your plans.*

"Yo trabajar para tu – por comida y casa a dormir?" I asked, smiling.

"Aqui? Para mi? – you work here for me?" he questioned, making sure he understood me.

"Si, si. Me gusta trabajar a la finca. Me gusta animales. Es trabajar verdad."

"Cuantos dias?"

"No se…Un dia… dose…Si esta bien… Un semana… No se."

He gazed out over the farm thinking over my preposition,

"Si, esta bien. Grab your bag." He nodded his head smiling.

He led me across the driveway to the building I had guessed to be a guesthouse. Upon entrance, I could see it was an office- a much older building with a desk, a chair, computer, and an old worn out couch which appeared to have started off as white, but was now a light brown due to the "dirt" and dust. The floor had a layer of dried "mud."

"Aqui. Dormir. I come back in one hora," he told me.

I wrapped myself in my sleeping bag and my body quickly shut down.

"Mi amigo, Mi amigo, aqui." I woke to see the farmer standing next to the couch, holding a bottle of tea and a small plastic container of food.

"Gracias, Gracias."

Feeling extremely grateful, I opened the container to find a small portion of lettuce, olives, chicken, and queso.

Eating the lettuce and olives, I handed him back the container, "Muchas, muchas, gracias." He looked at the remaining food confused.

"You have no food. You still have hunger?"

"Si, pero esta bien. No come animales."

He smiled and shook his head, trying to make sense of this gringo.

"Let's go. Come with me to town. I need a tool."

"Va a Cañete?" I asked.

"Si, Cañete."

We hopped in his pick-up truck and started down the road toward Cañete. I couldn't help but smile as I looked out the window. We went flying by rows and rows of cornfields, past the same houses, graves. *You walked all of this.*

"Mi amigo, right now, we drive south. Last night you walked north. You walked the wrong way," he told me as we drove, smiling over at me.

I thought back to the woman who told me to walk this way, maybe she knew… If you would have walked south, you never would have met this farmer, now you have food and a place to sleep tonight.

"Wrong way?" I asked him, questioning his statement. "No such thing. Esta aqui."

We arrived in town and pulled up next to the shop where he could purchase his tool. Across the street, men were unloading a massive quantity of bags from the bed of a truck. I couldn't recognize the name or the brand printed on the bag, but it sparked my curiosity. When he returned, I asked the man, "Que es?"

"Es químicos for la finca."

"Ah.. químicos… muy mal, si? You no usar?"

He looked at me, for the first time, I could tell I offended him.

"Si. Uso. Es necesario," he responded, defending himself.

I dropped the subject, and we drove back to the farm.

"Cuantas personas trabajar para tu? I asked as we pulled back into the farm.

"18."

"Esta bien," I looked out over the cornfields, which extended much further than I realized the night before. "Todo es tu finca?"

"Si."

"Corn por toro?"

"Si"

"Cuantos animales?"

"220."

"Wow, muy bien." I replied, remembering Eco Truly, "Mucho potential, to necesitas un bed and breakfast… you can have visitors from around the world come help on your farm. You teach them how to work the land, give them good food and convert the office into nice bedrooms."

Again he smiled. "Si?" He asked.

"Si."

He pulled out his phone to use translator to continue the conversation. I discovered he had two daughters around my age, both in college, and he was curious about my family.

"What did your parents say about the trip?"

"I didn't tell them."

"No phone? You don't call them?"

"Phone is in LA."

"What if something happens to you?"

"If something happens. Something happens. Nothing they can do from Florida. I will either see them again at Christmas or I wont."

He just stared at me.

"Loco."

"What do you want to do at the farm?" he asked.

"Anything, I worked with animals, with crops, I just want to learn."

"Can you drive tractor?"

Tractor! Hell yeah. Ever since I was a kid I really wanted to drive one of those big green tractors. This is dope.

"I have never driven before, but I'd love to learn."

"I'll teach you." He smiled at my excitement. "Go find Anna, up in the office. She will tell you what to get started on."

Back up in the office, a Peruvian girl in her mid 20s greeted me.

"Follow me," she said, smiling at me.

We walked down past the first pen of cows, fenced in lying around, and "mooing." As we continued down the path, I could sense a bit of commotion coming from a second pen, just up the road.

We continued walking. I could feel the energy shift, the mooing was louder, and the cows were making noises I was not used to hearing. In the air,

I could smell the smoldering of ashes and hot metal. In the distance I could see the pen, a group of men standing in the middle, the cows dispersed around the perimeter as if they were trying to avoid them. Next to the group of men was a smoldering pile of hot coals and a few metal rods heating above them. The smell became stronger and had strong hints of burning flesh and hair. I felt a pit rising in my stomach. *Oh no, no. They're not branding the cows are they? This is not what I signed up for.*

I got closer, reaching the fence, the cries of the cows got louder. I cringed.

"Are they branding them?" I asked Anna.

She looked at me confused, not understanding my English. She hopped the outer fence and motioned me to do the same.

As we walked toward the group of men I watched as a bull lay there on the ground in front of me, a rope tied tightly around its neck, another rope tied tightly around its hooves, binding its legs. It lay there helplessly on its side as one of the men stood over it, with his boot pressing into its neck. It cried out in pain. The mooing got louder and louder as if it were yelling at the men, pleading, "Stop! Please Stop! "

The moaning and crying intensified as another man approached with a large contraption. It had two hefty, wooden handles attached to two blades – like an over sized pair of scissors. The man walked over to the head of the bull. The man with his boot on the neck pressed harder, cutting off the air supply. Snot and saliva oozed from the nostrils of the cow at it lay there, gasping for breath. The man placed the sharp contraption near the base of the skull. The bull started shaking as he cut into the scalp, removing its horn with a loud cracking noise. Immediately, blood began squirting everywhere. There it lay yelling, panting, shrieking out of pain, its body convulsing as blood poured down its face.

The 4th man walked over with the hot piece of iron that had been heating over the coals. Now a glowing orange, he pressed the smoldering end of the rod onto the fresh wound of the bull – burning the open flesh wound at the base of its skull as tears began pouring down the animals face, mixing with the blood. The smell of burnt flesh again hit my nostrils. The men barked orders to each other in Spanish as they rolled him over- there was still another side to do.

I turned my head, not knowing if I could stand by and watch as this continued. Boot in place firmly on the neck, rope tightly in place, the man clipped the other horn. More blood squirted into the air as the blade cut deep into the skull. Again, the man pressed the hot iron onto the open skull wound of the animal as it gasped for breath, crying, screaming, and blowing snot out of its nostrils. As soon as the burning was finished, they untied the rope binding its legs. I watched as the young bull, covered in its own blood, took its remaining strength to stumble back up on its legs.

I just stood there, near the fence.

The men took the rope, made a lasso, and began lassoing their next victim.

After two failed attempts, they got one. Knowing his fate, the young bull fought with all his might, but he was no match to their system. They quickly had him on the ground, legs tightly bound, rope tight around his neck. The men stood there around the bull, the man again pressing his boot into the windpipe. They waved me to come over. I shook my head. *No, no, no.* They continued to wave me over, holding up the dangerous contraption as if to say, "You're turn, amigo."

"No, no, no." I said shaking my head, staying near the fence.

The group started talking loudly amongst each other in Spanish.

"Come!" the one man called.

After a few moments, I could tell they weren't really asking. This ceremony would not continue until I walked over. I walked towards the group, getting closer to the men and the animal that lay there on the ground, the one still extending the clippers in my direction.

"Why are you doing this?" I asked.

"Horns, bull, very dangerous," the one man replied "Angry bull, very dangerous." The man made a pair of horns with his two fingers and demonstrated them hitting his other hand as the other men around him laughed and made jokes.

"You. Your turn," holding the pliers out right in front of me.

I looked down at the cow, just laying there a few feet from me, gasping for breath as the man pushed in on his windpipe.

"No. No. I can't."

The man turned, and without hesitation, placed the clippers at the base of the skull and chopped off the horn with a large chunk of flesh. Blood squirted everywhere, oozing into the eyeball of the bull as it yelled, moaned, mucus shooting from its nostrils, its body shaking, going into shock.

They bore the hot iron straight onto the wound. This time, I watched the eye of the animal. It looked as if it were going to pop out of its socket as the hot iron singed its flesh. There was so much pressure so much pain, the eye watering up, tears, mixed with blood, pouring down its face.

I turned and walked back to the fence where Anna was watching.

"I can't do this. Is there something else… some other job I can do?" I asked her. "Anything?" *My stomach, my heart, my brain, and my body it could not make sense of what I was experiencing.*

"Come with me."

We left the second pen and entered through the feeding trough, a long narrow road lined on both sides by feeding animals. I walked down the isle observing the cows, most of them looked sickly with mucus dripping from their nostrils, eyes glazed over in an almost zombie state - no one home, mindlessly chomping away on the feed. I could feel the sadness. I noticed some of them had names written on their tags. I tried to communicate, say hello, and get some type of emotional response, nothing. Then, I remembered the bull at Eco Truly - the one that would wag his tail whenever we came over to his pen - the one that thanked me for cleaning his pen by licking my hand. *This is the same animal, yet this is not the same animal.*

We got to the end of the trough where there was a third gated pen. Again I heard the sounds of crying cows, moaning, yelling. They were all huddled together in the corner of the pen, squishing each other, trying to be the one furthest away from the three men standing near the back of the group. *This can't be good. They're all trying to run away.*

We reached the fence. "Watch. Giving vaccine," she instructed.

I watched as a man approached one of the cows in the back line, reached for his tail, and raised it high in the air. As he did this, the animal attempted to run forward, pushing further into the heard in front of him. The man followed a few steps, re-gripping the tail, lifting it higher into the air as the cow defecated all over him. The man took a large needle attached to a syringe and shoved it into the anus of the cow, injecting a fluid. The cow wailed, and defecated again, onto the hand and the boots of the man.

As he removed the needle, another man went behind the same cow, bearing a different needle and cartridge. The cow tried to move, escape, but it was trapped. The man injected the second needle into the anus of the cow and withdrew a small cartridge worth of blood, and he handed to a 3rd man who was standing nearby with a clipboard, organizing the samples. Once the cow had its blood taken, they sprayed a blue dot on the tail with spray paint and moved them to a neighboring pen.

I looked over at Anna "Just watch," she told me as she walked away, leaving me with the 3 men.

I stood there at the fence and looked on as the three men continued to shove needles in the anus of the cows. The cows were mooing, crying, and defecating everywhere, all over the men, all over each other - terrified, sad, and miserable. After finishing with a group, I watched the one walk away slowly, exiting to the neighboring pen. He looked at me. Making eye contact. He just stared at me. I felt as if he were saying, *"How can you just stand there? How can you just stand there and watch this happen? Can't you see I'm crying? Can't you see I'm suffering?"*

There was cow shit everywhere, everywhere, EVERYWHERE. It was all over the men, their boots, the fence, the needles, their hands, and their clothes.

Anna returned a few minutes later with some sweet rolls and bottles of soda. The men took a short break from their activity. I watched as the men slugged down the bright orange soda pop and wiped out the bag of sweet rolls. The one man grabbed the large 2-liter bottle, held it up to me in his shit-covered hands..

"Quiero? – you want?"

"No. Gracias."

After their snack, the men resumed their job, shoving needles into the anus of the cows. I had reached my limit.

Dude, you cant just stand by and watch this. What are you doing here?

I have a guy willing to feed me and give me a place to sleep. Once I leave. I'm on my own again, no food, no water, no place to sleep.

What are you willing to do for food and shelter? This? Are you willing to do this, to these animals?

I walked back to the office, back to Anna.

"I need to speak with Jose – necesito hablar con Jose."

"Tienes hombre? Lunch, almuerzo?"

"No, I just need to talk to him – solo necessito hablar con Jose. "

She called Jose and I met him on his back porch – where we had first met each other a few hours prior.

"Michael! Cómo estás," he greeted me with a

warm smile.

"Necessito hablar con tu."

"Primero, almuerzo! Anna! Aqui. Por Almuerzo, para Michael y tu." He handed Anna some soles to go get lunch for the two of us.

"No. No come almuerzo," I told him.

"Por que?" he looked at me confused.

The emotions from the past few hours coming out, I swallowed and breathed deeply,

"I can't work here.. No puedo trabajar aqui.."

His mood began to shift. He looked at me, handing me his phone with the translator app opened. He wanted an explanation.

I typed,

"My friend. I cannot work here. I love animals and your animals are all very sad. I cannot stay here. Thank you for offering a place for me to stay. I must continue my journey."

He read the message and continued to stare at his phone. He looked up at me, his eyes a bit glassy, a more somber Jose than I had experienced before.

"You go?"

"Yes."

He stood there for a moment, staring out over his farm.

"Now?"

"Yes."

He walked me to the office where my bag was. He looked very sad and in very deep thought.

"Where you go?"

"Cusco."

"Pan-American South. That way," pointing down the road.

"Gracias, Jose."

We shook hands. In that moment I knew. *He understands. It's no coincidence you ended up on his porch, in the middle of Cañete, Peru.*

I walked down the driveway, out the gate I had hopped the night before, turned left, and continued my trek to the Pan-American South, to Ica, to Cusco…

9 SUR

Day 20 Continued: November 27th

Back on the road again, I passed an older woman carrying a large bag of fruits. *Anything you can do to share energy.* I carried her bag for her then continued north until I hit the Pan-American South, just a few short miles from the farm.

I made my way down the entrance ramp, walking along the shoulder. It felt good to be on the road again. *You made the right decision, to leave the farm, the shelter, and the food.*

Reaching the main road, I continued south by foot, pausing whenever I heard the sound of a truck approaching so I could stop and throw up my thumb. I made it about a half mile down the road before an old, worn down truck pulled off on the shoulder, about 30 yards in front of me. *Victory!* I thought, running up to the passenger door. An older man and the strong odor of dead fish greeted me as I opened the door.

"Hola amigo, Donde Va?" he asked.

"Ica!"

He waved me in.

"Va a Pisco, 90km south. Bien?"

90 km closer to Ica, closer to Cusco.

"Si. Si. Muchas Gracias." I replied climbing up to the truck. As I closed the door, a screw from the side mirror popped off, leaving the contraption dangling.

The man smiled and laughed. "Esta Bien."

I had caught wind. We were moving fast. Next stop Pisco.

My new friend and I exchanged stories. He was carrying fish to sell at the market in Pisco. His name was Julio, 65 years old, a Lima native who adored his family and children. He asked about my parents, siblings and my experience in Peru. I told him of my journey so far. He began laughing.

"No bring money?" he said through his laughter.

"Si," I smiled. "No necessito."

"Loco Americano! Loco! Loco!" as he continued chuckling.

"Qué piensan tus padres?"

"No decir me padres" I said with a smile, letting him know I didn't tell them.

"Loco….. Tu.. Loco."

Construction on the Pan-American South caused us to take a little detour. After the previous nights walk, I could feel the anxiety building in me as we left the main road. We reached an intersection near the outskirts of Pisco. Julio pointed left "Ica," signaling it was time for us to part ways.

"Gracias Amigo! Adios!"

I was back on foot, bandana over my face, sun blazing down from above, I continued my journey step by step. My body was tired, but I had momentum. I walked a few miles before reaching a main intersection with signs pointing to Ica. My energy levels were low, without much rest or a real meal since I had left the temple, my body was yelling at me threatening to shut down.

There were buses, cabs, and trucks… *Jackpot*.

As I walked through the intersection, a mini van was loading with people.

"Ica! Ica! Ica!" The driver called.

"Mi amigo, no tengo soles pero… me puedo va con tu a Ica.. y… cuando.. es..full… yo salir" I did my best to ask if I could ride to Ica and hop out if the van filled up.

He hesitated, "No soles?"

"No mi amigo. Solo hitch hike." I raised my thumb. "Yo salir cuando tu tiene mucho personas,"

I pleaded in my poor Spanish.

"Ehh.. Esta bien," he patted my back nudging me in the van.

"Gracias. Gracias. Muchas Gracias."

I found a seat squeezed in the back, my body almost immediately shutting down. I felt immense gratitude. *I've got a place to sit in the shade, a nap, a ride to Ica, all in one, a little slice of Heaven.* I drifted off.

I felt someone shaking my body. "Aqui, Aqui, Ica!" the man next to me nudged me. I opened my eyes and looked around. We were in a garage.

Shit! Shit! Shit! You slept the whole way. You're off the main road, in some garage, somewhere. Find the main road. Find the Pan-American South.

Still in a daze I asked the driver "Pan-American South?"

"Ica! Aqui! Last stop."

"Donde Pan-American South?" I asked as I climbed off the van and grabbed my bag.

The man pointed down the street.

"Cuantas Kilometers?" I asked.

"Ehh… Dos"

"Gracias."

Thank God, 2 km.

I began walking, my body still not fully awake from my nap. I stumbled down the road. Stopping every hundred feet or so to regain my senses, bending over, hands on my knees, exhausted. My body did not want to wake up… My body did not want to move. *You're alright man. You're alive. Breathe. Just breathe.*

I had made it to Ica, but it was no time to celebrate. *You're still nearly 1000 km from Cusco, shelter, and your next meal.* I pulled out my map. I had to continue south. Next stop, Nazca.

Get out of downtown. No one will pick you up in the city. There are too many cab drivers. Walk out of the city.

Walk?! Walk!? I'm so tired. I need fuel. We've been trekking for miles and miles.

Come on. We don't have another option right now. One step at a time.

Continuing, slowly, I reached the main intersection of town. The Pan-American South ran straight through the central plaza. Still coming to my senses, I asked a man standing next to me on the corner, "South? Sol? Nazca?"

He pointed to the right.

"Gracias." I continued my trek.

My bandana covering my face, blocking the sun on my left, I walked, keeping my head down to avoid the sun as much as possible. I walked and I walked, and I walked, occasionally stopping for a few moments to rest, catch my breath, and give myself a pep talk.

I don't want to walk anymore. I don't. I want to eat. I want to rest. I'm tired. I'm really, really tired.

No. Stop. We have to keep moving. We have to walk out of the city. You want to eat? We have to get to Cusco.

Feeling extremely low on energy, I tried getting the attention of a few drivers, attempting to hitch. *No dice keep walking.* As I turned to get the attention of a truck passing, I saw a bus with a sign on the front left window that read "Lima." *No, that can't be right. I'm walking south. Lima is north.* On the next block in front of me, was a man standing on the corner of a used car lot.

"Mi amigo!" I got his attention and pointed in the direction I had been walking. "Nazca?" I asked pointing straight ahead.

"Lima," he replied

He pointed behind me, in the opposite direction.

"Nazca."

I pointed where he was pointing, where I had just come from, in disbelief, "Nazca!"

"Si. Si. Nazca."

"Gracias."

Shit. Shit. Shit. No. No.

I had just spent the majority of the afternoon walking north out of Ica. The sun was now beginning to disappear behind the buildings.

Alright man, you can either sit here and cry about it, or you can cross the road and start walking.

I crossed the road and continued my trek, going south. My mind raced as I walked back down that same road. *We wasted energy. We wasted fuel. We wasted so much fuel. You don't have food.*

As I walked down the road I watched a man pull out of his garage. He put on his blinker- he was heading south, toward downtown.

"Mi amigo! Mi amigo! Mi amigo!" I got his attention as I ran toward his window.

"Va Sol? South? Ayer?" I pointed down the road.

"..Si.. " he responded, confused.

"Va con tu.. I go with you?"

"No.. no.. no," he said, not really sure what was going on.

"Mi amigo," I pointed at the empty passenger seat, "Por favor."

He reached over, hesitating,

"Donde va?" he asked.

"Nazca," I replied.

He looked at me like I had two heads.

"Nazca! No! No. No. Solo voy downtown."

"Si. Si. Porfavor. Downtown es perfecto."

He opened the passenger door, and waved me in.

"Gracias"

"Why you no use cab?"

"No usar soles"

"Por que?"

"Un experimente. Leave wallet, dinero in LA."

I briefly explained as we drove south, back to the central plaza, down the blocks I had just walked.

We reached downtown, and the man pulled over to the side of the road. As I exited the vehicle, the man handed me 7 soles.

"No. No por favor. Gracias. No necesito." I told the man, handing them back.

He put his hands in the air, not willing to accept them back.

"Por favor.. para comida."

"No. No. necessito, please, here."

The man kept his hands in the air. He would not take them back.

It was the first time I had touched money in over 20 days. I didn't know what to do. I left the car and continued walking. I felt like I had sinned, like I had cheated. I felt guilty. Part of me wanted to throw them. *Why did he give this to me? I don't need this.*

The sun had set and darkness was quickly coming over the city as I walked south on the main highway. For a few miles I trekked, pausing to get the attention of trucks, buses, all failed attempts. *Please, please, can we stop this? Can we just lay down somewhere -In an alley? Here by the road? Anywhere.* I stopped on the side of the road and looked around, scouting for a place to sleep.

I spotted a bus stopped at a stoplight a few lanes over, the sign on the front windshield read "Nazca."

On impulse, I ran over to the bus to catch it before the light changed. The driver opened the back door. I entered the bus as the light turned green and the vessel continued moving south. I made my way up to the front where the driver was sitting.

"Nazca?" I asked.

"Si. Nazca."

 "Ocho soles."

I opened my palm showing him the 7 soles

from my friend.

"Esta bien," he signaled back towards the cabin with his thumb, inviting me to board.

I took a seat in the back cabin. My body didn't know what to do. I was hit with waves of extreme emotion, excitement, exhaustion, hunger, everything I had been pushing through the past few days, all coming up. *Shelter! A Place to rest! Thank God I have a place to rest for the next few hours. I will be in Nazca by tonight.*

I opened up my backpack and took out the remaining clementine from the devotee in Lima. *This is it. You've been saving this.* Every bite, every little sliver was like ecstasy, my body feeling so grateful for the nutrition and hydration. As I finished, I could feel my anxiety rising. *This bus ride won't last forever. Once the bus stops, it will be dark and you will be alone on the streets of Nazca. It will be too late to hitch a ride and you will be left sleeping in the streets. Enjoy this ride, enjoy it, it will be over before you know it.* I looked out the window as we passed desserts, mountains, cliffs, and roads with no shoulder. Physically, my body shut down, it was resting, but it was not a deep sleep, my mind still ran with anxiety. *I don't want this bus to stop. I don't want to go out in the cold.*

Before I knew it, I heard the hissing of the brakes. The doors opened, "Nazca! Nazca! Nazca!" the bus driver called.

I climbed off the bus. Before I reached the end of the block, a girl selling bracelets approached me,

"No Gracias."

"Please, please, no tengo dinero por comida," she said putting on a puppy dog face. She was quite an attractive girl - small, petite, long dark hair, and tan skin- reminding me of a girl I used to go to school with.

I smiled, "Yo tambien." I reached in my back pocket and pulled out the two bracelets that I had made as gifts for my mother and sister when I was in Eco Truly.

Her eyes lit up.

"Hace bracelets tambien," I explained in my Spanglish, "Yo traveling con zero dinero."

She got excited and called to her friend who was lingering behind.

"Ah my friend.. where are you from?" a guy about my age greeted me in a thick Columbian accent, speaking much better English than his female companion.

"Estados Unidos."

"Traveling without money?" he asked overhearing our conversation.

"Si."

"Very good. Very good. So do we, but we sell and juggle. We are going now to plaza to perform and make money. Want to join? You hang with us tonight?"

"I don't sell, but I will come sit, and hangout at the plaza."

"How do you live if you don't sell?"

"Solo mi energía."

"Hm.. Where are you sleep tonight?"

"No se.. maybe the parque on a bench. Y tu?"

"We are going to sleep at our friends garage. You can join us. If you like."

"Gracias. Gracias." *New amigos.*

I spent the night hanging out with the gypsies. They had met each other a year and a half ago on the streets of Medellin, and had been traveling together since then.

They performed in the plaza and made 37 soles in about an hour. We walked together down the road, stopping at a liquor store so they could purchase some tequila. We then stopped near an alley with street food and benches. My friends got a massive plate of stir fry, cooked with chicken. They offered me some, but I declined. There was a small container of dried corn kernels that came as a topping. "My friend, eat."

I squeezed a lime over the kernels and enjoyed every single one.

We were joined by two other travelers, which they had met in a previous city. The five of us sat there at a table, on a side street in Nazca. I did my best to translate their questions and conversation. It was near midnight. My friends had finished their tequila, and it was time to call it a night.

"We have early morning, our driver leave at 3:30 for Arequipa. Michael, let's go to garage and get some rest. A lot of trucks there. You will find your way to Cusco."

We walked 2km out of town and reached a building near a parking lot full of tractor-trailers. The building structure was an L shape, and my new friends began laying their blankets down in the sidewalk, nestled in the corner.

"Aqui? Outside?" I asked, under the impression we were sleeping inside the garage, on the other side of the wall.

"Si mi amigo. Better than a Hilton," he joked.

I had never slept on a sidewalk, let alone at truck stop in Peru.

"Si? Easta Bien? No peligroso?"

"Si. Si. Si." He laughed sensing my hesitation.

I laid out my sleeping bag there on the sidewalk.

"Can you wake me when you depart?"

"Si. Claro. Good night."

"Goodnight."

I climbed into my sleeping bag, resting there on the hard cement. *It's kind of like camping. Look you've got amigos and you're outdoors. It's not that bad.* My body was exhausted and I quickly drifted off to sleep on the sidewalk.

10 COMPAÑERO

Day 21 November 28th

"Michael, Michael, we leave for Arequipa."

I hopped out of my sleeping bag and wished a safe travel to my new friends.

"Hitch swiftly and quickly. May there always be wind in your sails," he blessed my journey.

"Adios."

It's 3:30 AM, I know you're tired, but let's move. You can sleep when you hitch.

From my map of Peru, I could tell that I had two options. There was a major route cutting through the mountains from Nazca east to Cusco. The other major route was continuing south to Arequipa, around the mountains, and up to Cusco. The second option added an additional 420km or 250 miles. *Straight to Cusco, we're going straight to Cusco.*

The truck engines in the lot began firing up as the drivers were preparing to start their day. I walked around the lot approaching the drivers.

"Cusco? Cusco?"

"Lima. Lima. Lima." All the drivers at this stop were heading north.

You have to find the road to Cusco.

I walked though the streets stopping at multiple gas stations along the way, searching for the right road leading out of Nazca to Cusco. Following the directions of strangers along my path, I was led through downtown, making a series of turns, until I came to a fork in the road. Massive trucks with trailers were parked lining both of the roads. In the median of the two roads was a small market and a few restaurants for truck drivers.

A man walked by me on the sidewalk.

"Mi Amigo, Donde Cusco?"

He pointed up to the road veering left. Then clapped his hands and whistled as he signaled a sharp left.

I followed the directions, walking up the road to the left, past the restaurant. The road ended, coming to a T. There was a large green sign with an arrow pointing left that read "CUSCO 660 km." *Bingo! This is perfect. It's early. You'll just catch a driver once he's done with his breakfast.*

One after another, the trucks turned down the

road. The hours began passing. *Maybe they don't see you.* I tried moving around the intersection. I noticed most of the trucks turning down the road were carrying gas with large labels over their trailers, "Peligroso." I sat in the shade of a small corner store, speaking with the Madre. She had been watching my failed attempts for hours.

"Keep trying," she told me. I had a cheerleader.

After another hour or so I found myself still standing on that corner. It was beginning to get hot. "CUSCO 660km," stared back at me. *A few hours have passed and you are exactly where you were. You can't depend on a ride. You've got feet right? Stop depending on other people to do things for you.* The song from "Santa Claus is Coming to Town" popped into my head:

"Put one foot in front of the other,
And soon you'll be walking cross the floor.
Put one foot in front of the other,
And soon you'll be walking out the door!"

I began walking down the road, pausing to smile and throw up my thumb whenever I heard the sound of a truck approaching from behind. There was no wind, no stops, and then a man on giant motorized cart came cruising down the road. His vehicle looked like a motorcycle with a cart attached to the back - a giant three-wheeled scooter, carrying scrap metal. I saw the vehicle and the man with his long hair blowing in the wind. Laughing to myself, I threw my thumb up. *Why not?* He pulled off to the shoulder of the road, and nodded his head, signaling me to hop in the back.

"Donde va?" I asked, hopping into the cart.

"Ehh.. 20km," he replied.

"Gracias Amigo," I replied, as I shuffled around in the cart, trying not to get shanked by the array of sharp metal objects I was sharing a ride with.

I sat there, carefully crouched, watching the road zip by, smiling. *This is so much faster than walking. 20 km you don't have to walk.*

Up ahead, on the side of the road, I spotted a man in a turquoise sweatshirt with his thumb in the air. The driver again pulled off to the side of the road, signaling the traveler to join me in the back cart. He was an Asian looking guy in his 20s. I couldn't believe it. *Another hitchhiker, on the same road - this must be the right route.*

As he began shifting around in the metal, trying to find a safe place to sit, he asked,

"Hitchhike? Travel?"

"Si, yes, yes."

"Where you go?"

"Cusco," I replied with a smile.

"Cusco? Tu? You go Cusco?" He pointed at me.

"Si."

"Cusco," he pointed at himself.

We both started laughing as we sat in the back of the small cart, over 650km away from our destination.

"Soy de Japan."

"Estados Unidos, What is your name?"

"Masuru and you?"

"Michael."

I sat there in the open cart with my new friend from Japan. The wind blew strong on my face as we passed by farms and ancient archaeological sites. I couldn't help but think of the MasterCard commercials...*Priceless*.

Heading out of the city and into the desert, we reached a weigh-in station for trucks. Our driver pulled over, and we hopped out there on the side of the road. My new Japanese companion and I sat there sharing stories, taking breaks in conversation whenever we would hear a truck approaching in the distance.

30 minutes turned to an hour, 1 hour turned to 2. The sun was beating down from above and we were both getting roasted. There was a woman with a small tent about 25 yards off the side of the road up ahead. She was selling sweets and Cola to the drivers as they exited the weigh in station.

The two of us, feeling worn from the heat and the sun's rays, joined the woman under her tent, finding shade. Every time we would hear a truck, the three of us would leave the shade and walk out to the road. Masuru and I would raise our thumbs high in the air as the woman waved her bottles of Inca Kola. The traffic was slow, sometimes it would be 10, 15 minutes before a car would drive by. It was quiet, and hot. *You started at 3:30 this morning, almost 11 hours ago, and you've only made it 20km out of the city. You could be walking.* I looked at my map - Puquio was the next major city, over 150km away, up through the mountains.

"Masuru, maybe we walk."

Looking up ahead, the road did not look promising for pedestrians as it zigged and zagged sharply with no shoulder.

"Stay here. Walk is dangerous."

Another truck pulled out of the weigh station, as the three of us lined the road. The man called the woman over. He was thirsty.

As the woman was finishing her sale, I approached the side window,

"Mi amigo, donde va?"

"Chuquimaran." It was a city, but it was not on my map.

"Puquio?" I asked.

"No. no."

"Cuantas km on this road?" I pointed straight.

"Cuantas km mas?"

"Ehh.. 80 km mas."

"We join you?" I pointed at Masuru and at his truck.

He hesitated, "Mountains mucho frío," he replied, trying to talk us out of it.

"Esta bien, Esta bien."

He waved us in.

For the next hour we drove up through the mountains, along winding roads lined with steep cliffs. Graves lined the sharp turns, reminding of the dangers of traveling such a trail. We went from cactus and desert to tundra, goats, and llamas. We climbed higher, and higher up the mountains. *This is beautiful, absolutely beautiful.*

Reaching the apex of the mountain, there was a small town consisting of about 8 buildings, half of which were restaurants for truckers.

"Aqui." The driver stopped and unlocked the doors.

As I climbed down from the cabin, I was immediately hit with a freezing chill from a large gust of wind. I quickly layered up with my long sleeve and pullover. My body shivered as it struggled to adjust to the new environment.

Masuru was hungry. We stopped at one of the restaurants offering lunch, and I watched as he ate his plate of rice with a chicken leg, covered in a brown sauce. I was just thankful to be out of the cold. When he finished, we were back on the side of the road, thumbs up to hitch out next ride to Puquio.

I stood there on the side of the road, thumb in the air, as the wind and cold cut through my layers. The trucks continued to blow by. I noticed the locals in the town were all bundled in winter jackets, wearing gloves and thick hats to cover their ears. *Why didn't you bring a jacket, you idiot*, I thought to myself as I jumped up and down trying to generate some body heat. Masuru, standing next to me, began sniffling and coughing violently. It sounded like phlegm was coming deep from his throat.

Up there on that mountain, time seemed to be different, like a weird twilight zone. The seconds felt like minutes, the minutes like hours. My body screamed every time a gust of wind blew, chilling my bones. What felt like a week, was 2 hours with no stop, no hope of the next ride. I continued standing there with my thumb raised, my mind racing. *I'm here on this mountain, this kid next to me is sick, and getting worse every minute. No trucks are stopping, You have no food. It's too cold to sleep up here without shelter. You're at rock bottom.* Then as if the gods were playing some sort of sick joke, I felt a drop of water on my head, then another, and another. *Shit. Shit. Shit…. Is that… yeah.. It's raining.*

"Masuru!" I called to my companion who was sitting on a step in front of the restaurant, still coughing, and spitting up mucus from his throat.

"We aren't gonna last long up here if this keeps up."

He just looked at me, waiting for me to present a better option. The sun had almost completely set and we had about 20 minutes before it got extremely dark as the temperature continued to drop.

I felt like I was living in the scene from LOTR:

The fellowship is climbing through the snowy mountains of the Pass of Caradhras and Sauromon murmurs "If the mountain defeats you, will you risk the more dangerous road" while he casts a spell causing the mountain to avalanche upon the fellowship. Gimlee proposes, "If we cannot pass over the mountain, let us go under it. Let us go through the mines of Moria."

"We gotta get off the mountain. We hitch back to Nazca, at least its warm enough to sleep there without shelter."

"Back to Nazca?" he questioned.

"Yeah I think were on the wrong route, not a lot of trucks," I showed him my map. "Nazca.. Arequipa," I explained.

"Arequipa?" he questioned, continuing his fit of violent coughing.

"Yes, Let's to it," I responded, reassuring my friend, "Arequipa."

There were a few trucks parked on the side of the road facing back toward Nazca, their drivers resting and re-fueling in the restaurant. We approached the first driver that returned to his vehicle.

"Va a Nazca?" I asked.

"Si," he responded as he began walking around his vehicle, clipping on large pieces of plastic above the tires.

"We come with you a Nazca?" Masuru added.

The man stopped what he was doing and looked at the two of us standing there in the rain.

He handed us a piece of plastic and smiled.

"Si. Si."

We assisted him in clipping on the plastic apparatus, and the three of us climbed into the cabin. Sheltered from the rain and the wind, a huge smile came across my face.

"Donde va? Nazca?" he asked, as he fired up his truck.

"Cusco.. well.. Nazca.. Arequipa.. Cusco."

"Va a Nazca y Chala esta noche," the man explained, telling us his route.

"Chala es sol de Nazca?" I asked still learning the geography.

"Si, Nazca.. Chala.. Arequipa."

We began cruising back down the winding road, along the cliffs, towards Nazca.

I watched as the rain poured down on the windshield. *I am so thankful to be in this truck right now, warm, covered from the rain.*

"You want to go to Chala?" he asked.

"Tonight?"

"Si."

I looked at my friend Masuru, a huge grin came across his face, unable to hold his excitement.

"Si, claro," I eagerly responded.

That front cabin became our home for the next few hours as we cruised through the night, down the highways of Peru. After a few stops, we reached the town of Chala around midnight. I began scouting places to sleep as we entered the town.

We pulled up to a truck stop and the three of us hopped out of the cabin to brush our teeth.

"Where are you guys sleeping tonight?" asked the driver.

"No se," I replied.

We grabbed our bags and thanked the driver for rescuing us from the cold, and getting us down to Chala.

"Gas station?" Masuru asked.

We were on the same frequency.

"Yes. Gas station, less than 1 km," I pointed down the road.

"Perfect."

Reaching the gas station, we were greeted by a large dog. He barked and growled at us, warning us that we were entering his territory. We began scoping out a place near the bathrooms to lay our sleeping bags as the dog followed us, barking and causing commotion.

Masuru reached in his bag, pulled out a dinner roll, ripped it in half, and gave it to the barking animal. His tail began to wag as he accepted the peace offering and ceased his barking. He sat there, smiling. We had just made a crucial friend, one to watch over us as we slept.

We found a corner, away from the trucks and gas pumps – near a stack of old truck tires. I laid my bag down on the cement near the tires, under a street lamp. Out of nowhere Masuru whips out a tent front his bag, like Mary Poppins. I stood there watching in amazement.

"Sleeps two," he told me.

I smiled at my Japanese friend, "Gracias. Gracias," thankful to have a bit of shelter.

We laid there in the tent at the gas station.

"Wake up 3:30?" I checked to make sure we were on the same page. His coughing continued and seemed to be getting worse. He held up his phone, showing me it was 12:30. He looked at me, not excited.

"3:30, tree tir-ty?" he repeated, in his Japanese accent, making sure he heard me right.

"Yes. If you can. Trucks leave early. Catch ride early. Arequipa tomorrow."

"Yes. Yes. Tree tir-ty, Arequipa." He smiled, still coughing. "I set alarm."

"I met you this morning," he continued as we lay in the tent, "Feels like 1 week."

11 FRIO

Day 22 November 29th

BEEP. BEEP. BEEP.

I awoke to the sound of the alarm.

No way. There is no way it's 3:30. I just fell asleep.

BEEP. BEEP. BEEP. The alarm continued.

"Masuru! Masuru!" I said in a loud whisper, waking my friend who was sleeping through the alarm.

He woke up, coughing.

"What time is it?" I asked.

He looked at his phone, turning off the alarm.

"3:30."

I know you're tired, I know you're hungry, but you can't show it. We have to keep moving. He's sick, he's really sick and has low energy, you gotta stay upbeat, I thought to myself.

I smiled and chanted "Arequipa! Arequipa! Mucho carro, muy rapido!"

I could see the energy returning to his body.

"Mucho carro! Mucho carro!" he chanted back between coughs.

We packed the tent, rolled our sleeping bags, and walked back to the truck stop. Trucks lined the road facing both directions. The drivers began waking and firing up their trucks. One by one, we approached each driver with a truck facing south. We watched as the road began to clear out. The drivers all continued their journeys, not wanting two new companions. The sun still hadn't fully risen.

"Its alright, it's still early." I told Masuru.

"Mucho Carro! Mucho Carro!" he chanted.

It was back to the classic hitch. Our thumbs went up as trucks cruised by past us, one after the other, after the other. It was near 5AM, the perfect hour for hitching. As we stood there, near the truck stop, on the side of the road, a red truck stopped along side. The driver rolled down his window - Latin Rock was blasting from his speakers.

He asked us something in Spanish. We looked at each other – neither of us understood.

"Arequipa! Arequipa!" we both chanted.

"Arequipa?" He asked reaching to unlock the door.

"Arequipa! Arequipa!" we repeated.

He reached over and opened the door. We quickly learned our new friend did not speak any English or Japanese, and he was not going to Arequipa.

"Camana!"

"Camina? I asked the man, looking over at Masuru who looked as confused as I felt.

"Si. Si. Camana. Camana... Camana... Arequipa"

"Ah, bueno," I understood. It was a city, south of here, on the way to Arequipa.

As we settled in, he cranked up the music. He began singing and dancing like he was the lead singer of the band as he slugged down a Volt energy drink. Music blasting, windows down, we were cruising down the highway getting closer to Arequipa, closer to Cusco, every minute.

I sat in the back, on the driver's bed, while Masuru sat shotgun. An empty energy drink bottle lay on the dash next to a giant, shiny, red, bag that read "Panetón." There was an image of a fluffy looking pastry with walnuts, raisins, and dried fruit. My mouth began salivating as my stomach growled, reminding me, *you haven't eaten in days.*

"Beautiful, look!" Masuru got my attention off the bread as he pointed out the window. We were driving down the coast, along massive cliffs which stood above the Pacific Ocean.

"Peligroso," the driver warned as we inched around a curve where a dozen or so gravestones marked the lives of those lost on similar journeys.

The driver's name was Juilan. He had been driving for over 14 hours straight when he picked us up. Over the next few hours, the three of us jammed out to Latin rock as we zipped down the Pacific coast. We would make the occasional pit stop to pee on the side of the road or to grab more Volt so Julian could have a little boost. We drove through tunnels, up mountains, through villages and farms until we reached the town of Camana.

We pulled off the main road and turned down a small alley. We stopped in front of a row of houses, one of which had the garage door opened.

"Vamos!" said Julian. We hopped out of the truck and were joined by four men who were waiting in the garage. The group of us quickly unloaded the furniture that was in the back of the truck into the garage.

We said goodbye to Julian, walked the few blocks back to the main road, and raised our thumbs up to continue on toward Arequipa. It was only noon and we were about 200km out from the city. Only a few minutes passed before a large truck, transporting cars, was pulled over in front of us on the side of the road.

"Arequipa! Arequipa!" we chanted, nearing

the passenger side.

The door opened.

"Si. Si. Arequipa."

We spent the afternoon hauling cars with our new friend on the way to Arequipa. Due to the heavy load, the truck moved at an extremely slow pace. The front cabin was hot - there was no ac, and not a lot of wind as we drove through the heat of the afternoon. However, we were moving, getting closer to Arequipa, closer to Cusco.

One of the devotees in Lima had given me the address to a temple in Arequipa during the Cocoa fiesta. The thought of having a meal and shelter for a night was starting to tease me. *We should continue on to Cusco, don't be soft. You can make it a few more days without food and shelter, come on.*

"Sleep in Arequipa tonight or continue straight on to Cusco?" I asked Masuru, leaving it to chance.

"Cusco," he replied. I smiled. I loved the drive.

"Cusco."

As we entered the city of Arequipa, our new friend pulled off to the side of the road. The driver instructed us to walk straight for 7km or so to reach the main road to Cusco.

We began walking, and my body quickly reminded me that it hadn't had food, water, or much sleep. Sitting was fine, but when I told my body to walk, it refused to cooperate. Each step felt like I was walking up a steep slope through sand. My legs burned and ached as my body broke down the muscle for fuel. Each step became it's own endeavor. *One step at a time. Come on, one step at a time.* My body refused to listen to me.

"Masuru, five minutes. I need to sit."

I sat on a ledge and reached for my canteen. *This water was from Eco Truly. You didn't drink it because of the traveling sickness. Are you sure you want to do this?* I opened the lid and through my cracked lips, took a sip of the questionable water. The water touched my lips and tongue. My body rejoiced. It had been almost two full days since my last drink in Cañete. *Glorious. This is glorious. This is amazing.*

Masuru, sitting on the ledge beside me, reached in his bag and handed me one of the old dinner rolls he had been stashing.

"Eat."

I shook my head not wanting to eat his food.

"You haven't eaten since I met you. Eat, please."

I took the roll. I held it.

"Thank you, Masuru. Thank you."

I took my first bite.

Holy shit.

Holy shit.

It was delicious.

I finished the roll and we continued walking. We hit the main intersection and positioned ourselves to be visible to the drivers leaving Arequipa en route to Cusco.

In good spirits, we stood on the corner attempting to hail our next ride. A man came over and approached us,

"Where are you guys going?"

"Cusco," we replied.

"I have van going to Yauri, Espinar. I can take you to Yauri if you like."

"Gracias, pero no tengo soles, I replied."

"Esta Bien. No necesitas. I take you to Espinar, if you like," the man smiled. "Leave in 30 minutes," he pointed to his van parked across the street.

"Gracias! Gracias!"

I pulled out my map to locate Yauri- Espinar.

The last thing you want is to be stuck in a small town in the mountains, freezing cold, with no jacket, and no truck traffic, AGAIN, I reminded myself.

Yauri was about half way between Arequipa and Cusco, however there was no major highway connecting the cities.

"We can take a risk on Yauri, getting halfway to Cusco tonight. We would only be a short distance to Sicuani. Looking at the map, worst case, a two-day walk. There's a main highway running from Sicuani to Cusco. It will be easy to hitch from there. The other option is to pass on the ride to Yauri and hope to catch a direct ride from here to Cusco," I explained to Masuru as we studied the map.

"You decide," he replied.

"Let's give it a go," I said, half sure of myself. "Yauri."

"Yauri," repeated Masuru, trusting the decision.

We boarded the van and found seats near the back. The van loaded up about 7 more passengers, and we took off for Espinar. Before we could make it out of Arequipa, flashing lights appeared behind us… Policia. With a quick check of our passports and a slight interrogation of the driver - we were back on the road, out of Arequipa, heading up into the mountains. I stared out the window, watching the sunset behind the mountains, the sky a bright orange, fading to pink to blue. *Better than any picture could do justice.*

With the disappearance of the sun and the change in altitude, in a matter of minutes the temperature seemed to drop at least 50 degrees. I began dozing off. I pressed my head against the window and immediately shot right back up. *Holy shit, wow, that's freezing.* I looked around the bus - everyone was wearing heavy, winter jackets, hats, and scarves. *Here you are with your thin little Under*

Armor fleece, you idiot. Seeing that I was ill prepared, the driver passed back a spare blanket that he had upfront.

We continued driving - it was now pitch black outside the van. Every minute, I felt it getting colder, and colder, and colder as we climbed higher and higher into the mountains. It was dark. I was tired, but I could not sleep. My body began to shake. *You have everything you need. You have everything you need*, I reminded myself.

I opened my bag, and put on all of the shirts and layers I had except for two t- shirts, which I used to wrap my neck and face. I sat there curled in the fetal position on the back seat, still shaking to get warm, unable to sleep as the van continued on toward Yauri, getting higher and higher and higher into the mountains.

Finally, my body shut down and I was able to get some rest.

"BANG!" It sounded like an explosion on the side of the road. The van pulled over to the shoulder and shut off. I sat up to observe the situation. Everything outside the van was pitch black. The driver began jiggling the keys to restart the engine again. I heard the engine cranking, cranking, cranking then die out.

He tried again. Cranking, cranking, cranking… nothing.

And again he turned the key - Cranking, cranking, cranking... nothing.

The man began yelling in Spanish.

Too tired to sit up and watch, I curled back into the fetal position trying to go back to sleep. *You're stuck, stranded, freezing, on top of a mountain in the middle of Peru. Yeah, you're right. I am… but at least I'm in a van. Do you realize how lucky you are that you are in this van? If you're so cold that you cant sleep and you are inside the van, image how cold you'll be when you're outside, when you get to Espinar.*

For the next three hours or so we rested in the broken down van. A rescue truck came and began loading passengers, however it could not fit everyone in one trip. Masuru and I would be on the second trip.

A while later, the driver came over telling us to exit the van. We grabbed our bags, leaving the shelter, going out into the frigid night. As we stood there, a man approached us,

"Rescue truck, 5 soles."

Shit. No. I looked around me. Darkness. Tundra. Nothing. If you sleep out here, you might not wake up.

"0 soles. Tengo 0 soles," I told the man.

He shook his head and walked away.

"What are we going to do?" Masuru turned to me.

"I don't know. I don't know"

"You have zero soles? Zero soles?" Masuru questioned me, hinting that if I was holding out, now was not the time.

"0," I told my friend. "You go."

We both stood there with our bags on the side of the road.

The van driver and the rescue man began talking in Spanish. The driver walked over to us.

"It's ok. You go. Both. Go. Can't leave you here. Too cold."

"Gracias. Gracias."

We slammed six people into the cabin of the pickup truck and continued to Yauri.

The rescue vehicle stopped outside a bus station. We had arrived in Espinar. I grabbed my bag and stood there on the sidewalk with Masuru, shivering, scouting for shelter. We made our way into the bus station, gaining shelter from the strong winds. Most of the booths at the station were closed, and the entire second floor was dark. We climbed the stairwell to the second floor, and set up Masuru's tent in an opening between 2 booths. I climbed in the tent, and crawled into my sleeping bag. I lay there bundled, anticipating the feeling of the sun on my skin the next morning. I thought back to those times in Mira Flores, walking, sweating, the sun beating down, *what I would do to trade places.* It was very early in the morning somewhere around 2AM. *Don't sleep in - trucks move early,* I reminded myself.

"Masuru, 5 AM?"

"Yes. 5. I set alarm."

"Goodnight."

"Goodnight."

12 PROMISE LAND

Day 23 November 30th

The alarm went off. *No, No, No. I'm just starting to feel warm. I want to go back to sleep.* I just lay there until I heard violent coughing. *Masuru is awake. His cough is getting worse. This temperature cannot be good for him. You gotta get him out of here.*

"Good morning!" I greeted him, knowing the importance of keeping good spirits.

"Good morning," he murmured, barely able to talk through the phlegm caught in his throat.

"How are you feeling?"

"Good. Good." We both smiled at his attempts to stay positive…

"Good. I'm glad to hear it. That's great news. Today Sicuani, then Cusco."

"Cusco, Cusco," he chanted in his Japanese accent.

We packed our gear, left the terminal, and asked the first person we saw for directions out of town, toward Cusco.

The sun was just beginning to rise as we made our way through the cobblestone roads of the beautiful town, following the instructions the stranger had given us. The roads were empty, dead.

"No mucho carro," my friend reminded me.

This felt like a very similar situation. There was no traffic and it was freezing.

"Let's keep walking. Worst case 2 days walk to Sicuani."

We walked out of town across a bridge as the sun continued to rise. *Yes! The sun!* I could feel its rays, heating my body through my clothes, reducing my chill.

As the buildings disappeared from sight, we found ourselves on a small road, weaving through the countryside. Although the situation seemed unfavorable, we were in good spirits. Singing, chanting, and joking, as we walked past rolling green hills, high up in the mountains. It was beautiful - green pastures and hills as far as the eye could see. As we continued walking, the road turned from pavement to gravel. We turned to each other and laughed in disbelief. We were 'hitchhiking' on a gravel road with no traffic - no trucks, no cars, and no buses - just green rolling hills and pastures with a few goats and llamas.

"This can't be it. This can't be the main road to Cusco," I told my friend.

Every 20 minutes or so a car would pass. We came to the conclusion that we probably weren't going to get another hitch until we reached Sicuani. We had about 70 km or 44 miles until we reached Sicuani.

I heard a vehicle driving through the hills behind us. As the car came around the corner, we moved out of the middle of the road and stood there with our thumbs up smiling. The car got closer and closer. Then it stopped right there in font of us in the middle of the road. It was a small black car reminding me of the cabs back in Lima.

No way. This must be a cab. I thought to myself. Looking at Masuru with disbelief.

The diver rolled down his window. Masuru went over to talk to the man. He turned back at me and waved me over. Thinking that there was probably just a miscommunication with the language barrier, I popped my head in the window.

"Mi amigo donde Va?" I asked the man.

"Sicuani." He replied.

"Sicuani?"

"Si. Si…Y tu? Donde?"

"Sicuani! Sicuani!" We both chanted.

He reached over and unlocked his doors.

"Come, Come!"

We looked at each other in disbelief, and started laughing.

"Where you go in Sicuani?" he asked as we settled in.

"We go Sicuani y then Cusco."

"Va a Cusco?" The man got excited.

"Si. Si. Start in Lima and hitchhike here. Go to Cusco."

"He smiled. Vive in Cusco! I go Cusco mas tarde."

"You go Cusco today?"

"Si. Si."

"I am principal at school in Sicuani. We have Spelling Bee today. Then Cusco esta noche."

"We go with you? To Cusco?"

"Si. Si. Claro. Vamos Cusco!"

"You hang out while I go to Spelling Bee. Then after, vamos a Cusco."

"Si. Si. Claro."

I looked back at Masuru. We had done it. We had met an angel on the side of the road in Espinar that came to our rescue. We were safe, and sitting in the car that would be taking us to Cusco. A deep feeling of relief came over me. *No more walking, no more nights in the cold.*

Our new friend Emil had backpacked South America in his 20s. As we drove down the road, we passed an archeological site with ruins. Emil parked the car and told us to go explore for a few minutes. It was my first 'tourist' experience of the trip. After our little pit stop, we continued through the countryside to Sicuani,

"Breakfast? You eat breakfast?"

"No." replied Masuru.

"You want breakfast?"

"Si. Si," Masuru replied.

"I'm ok," I added.

"We stop next town for breakfast."

We pulled over in the next town, which had one restaurant and a small corner store. We got out of the car and sat in the restaurant. *It's alright. Tonight you will have food. Tonight you will be in Cusco.*

Emil looked at us and smiled,

"I buy. I buy."

I looked at the plate of the people sitting at a nearby table. *Chicken.*

"Gracias, pero, no quiero." I told my new friend.

"Que! Por Que? No tienes hombre?"

"Pollo. No come pollo."

"Que? No come pollo?" he asked in disbelief.

"Si. Si." I laughed, "Esta Bien."

The woman came over to the table to take the order.

"Tres?" she asked.

"Solo dos," I replied. "No quiero, Gracias."

Emil looked at me in disbelief.

"No come carne? Nunca?"

"No."

"Que come? He asked."

"Frutas, vegetales, pan, granola."

"Que frutas?"

"Todos. Manzana, banana, mango. Todo."

"Quiero comprar tu comida," he told me.

After they finished their meal, Emil bought a bag of apples and water from the corner store across the street.

"Aqui."

"Gracias! Muchas Gracias!"

I sat in the car, sipping the water, and eating an apple as we continued on toward Sicuani, relaxing. *This is too good to be true. You are spoiled.*

As we entered the town of Sicuani, Emil turned and asked us,

"You want shower?"

"Shower?" I asked in disbelief.

"Si. Si. I have apartment here. We go before the Spelling Bee so I can change. You guys shower, change, hangout."

We parked the car on a small cobblestone road, entered a garage, and walked 2 flights of stairs up to his rooftop apartment.

I took off the clothes I had been wearing for the past five days, and hopped in the outdoor shower. I turned on the water, preparing myself for the frigid blast. *Warm water! You spoiled man.*

Standing there on his rooftop, I basked in the sun, drying off, looking down to the city and off to the mountains in the distance. Emil threw on his suit and was headed back down the stairs.

"You want to hangout here? Or come to Spelling Bee?"

I looked at Masuru who was sitting near the railing

on the roof, hunched over, looking the worst that I had seen him.

"Masuru. Esta bien?"

"No. No. My stomach. My stomach and my head." He said still coughing and spitting up mucus. Altitude sickness."

"You want to hang out here? We can stay."

"No. No. I'm ok. Let's go Spelling Bee."

"Alright. Emil. We will come to Spelling Bee."

Our new friend was excited that we were joining him at work. When we got to the high school, Masuru seemed to be in better spirits. We found 2 seats near the back of the gymnasium and watched as the smartest kids from schools around the area competed in the Spelling Bee.

During the competition I couldn't help but notice the words that these kids were learning - "Buy" "Sell" "Rich" "Poor" "Cash" "Fat."

The competition ended, and the three of us loaded back up into the car. Next stop- Cusco. Leaving Sicuani, we were about two and half hours out from our final destination. We drove through the valley as the clouds began opening up on us, releasing a downpour of rain.

I sat there, staring out the window. The landscape was stunning. We passed green mountains, lush with flora, and farms with cows grazing on the side of the road. I sat there feeling extremely grateful, reflecting on the past 6 days as the rain continued to pour down on the front windshield. *Tonight I will have shelter. Tonight I will have food.*

Every few minutes we would pass a woman on the side of the road, a native selling a mystery liquid in recycled cola bottles.

"Chicha," Emil explained as we drove past one of the woman.

"Chicha?"

"Alcohol drink made from corn. Like beer."

"Ahh, Chicha."

We continued driving, and the view out the window transitioned to slums, abandoned buildings, and barren lots – littered with rubble and debris. We were getting closer to the city, closer to industrialization. I felt myself getting excited, recalling all of the magnificent things I had heard about the sacred city, the Inca capitol.

As we drove, a red banner, advertising for a mobile carrier hung above the road, spanning both lanes of traffic reading "CLARO- Bienvenidos a Cusco." *Ah! Gracias, Claro. I can feel the culture, the rich history of Cusco really captured in this plastic banner.* We continued driving past shacks, rubble, and billboards while plastic bottles and other debris lined the sides of the road.

"Cusco, Welcome to Cusco." Emil looked over at the two of us. I continued to stare out the window, observing. Part of me was so excited. *I had just spent the last 6 days living on faith that I would arrive here. Faith that I would have food and shelter, and it was all so close.* Another part of me was a bit saddened. *I had heard so much about this ancient city, and all I see when I look out this window are the effects of consumerism - the slums, the people doing their best to transition to the industrial, corporate world around them, causing them to live like this. We went from peaceful, beautiful, farmland and – boom – slums, rubble, and pollution.*

We continued into Cusco toward the downtown area where Emil pulled off to the side of the road. There on the sidewalk, we said goodbye to our new friend, Emil, the angel.

Standing there on the sidewalk in Cusco, I looked over at Masuru,

"Cusco!"

"Cusco!" he celebrated, still hacking up a lung.

He decided to walk with me to the temple. I pulled out the piece of paper, the puzzle piece from Eco Truly. I remembered a conversation with Fabio in which he mentioned the temple being near one of the historic, central plazas. With no map we began walking, following the signs to the historic area.

Step by step, block-by-block, we trekked. The last few miles did not get any easier. Masuru's cough seemed to worsen. My legs didn't want to listen. Our bodies were both shutting down, struggling to adjust to the extreme change in altitude. I felt like Samwise and Frodo as they climbed the slopes of Mount Doom with the ring.

We reached the Plaza De Armas. I recognized it from the book I had been carrying on Peru. It was the central hub. *We have arrived – the statues, the cathedrals, and the cobblestone roads. I could feel the history. Hey, come on. Let's move. Food, shelter- the address - we're close.*

I looked at the piece of paper - I could not make sense of the address. I showed a local and we began walking in the direction he pointed. *I hope this place exists. I hope this place exists.*

We continued using the same strategy, asking locals every few blocks to make sure we were getting closer. We walked past cathedrals, down ancient roads, and through markets, reaching a small side street with the sign, "Queswa."

We walked up the steep, slopping cobblestone road, and reached the top where it intersected with the next road, "Alta Vista."

There was a man standing there on the corner. We showed him the piece of paper.

He smiled. "Aqui. Here."

I turned around to see a sign above the building behind us, "Yoga" "Templo."

It was real.

I opened the black gate in front of the door and eagerly knocked.

The large blue doors opened, and a young girl greeted us. She was wearing a white dress with a shawl over her head and shoulders,

"Hola. Hare Krishna," she uttered softly.

"Hola! Hola! Hare Krishna!"

"Can I help you?" she asked in broken English.

"Si, si. I am looking for Mahakala. Travel here from Eco Truly in Lima," I showed her the piece of paper in my hand with the address and the name "Mahakala."

Confused, she told us to sit down, and she would call Mahakala.

"He will come in few minutes. Do you want something to drink?"

"Si gracias."

She returned with a metal mug, filled with a warm pineapple tea.

A few moments later, a man about 30 years old entered the temple. He was wearing socks with his sandals, a faded orange robe and his head was shaved except for the same small patch near the crown of his head. Over his shoulder, he carried a small satchel. With a large smile and open arms he greeted me,

"Cómo estás! Viaje de Eco Truly? Si?"

I stood up, hugging the stranger.

"Si Si. This is my new friend Masuru. I met on trip here from Eco Truly."

"En Espanol? Hablas?"

"Un poco. Es mi amigo Masuru, en route aqui, en Nazca, en carro, Masuru," I attempted to explain.

"Ah Bueno... Voluntario?"

"Masuru, do you want to volunteer?"

He coughed. He was hesitant... "Tonight? Just tonight?"

"Solo una noche?" I asked Mahakala.

"Una, dos, tres, no es importante."

"Si. El quiere."

"Michael, va a la finca? Tu va a la finca a Sabado? Bien?"

"Si. Si. La finca," I told him I would be going to the farm on Saturday.

"Bueno."

"Mahakala, aqui, para tu, the temple," I gifted him the remaining four apples from Emil, my only food source for the return trip.

"Ah! Gracias Michael!"

"Ven! Su casas."

He brought us in past the kitchen, up a flight of stairs to a small common area where we removed our shoes. There was a small sign that read "Ashram de Devotees," next to two small swinging doors, the kind you would find at the entrance of an old western saloon. We entered the bedroom, a large room with a window and three bunk beds.

"Michael, Masuru, Aqui y aqui," he pointed to two top bunks, "Bien?"

"Si. Si. Muchas Gracias."

I put down my bag and hopped up on the bed.

"Tengo hombre?" Asked Mahakala. "Quiere Prasada?"

"Si. Prasada, Muchas muchas gracias."

We followed him back downstairs to the main room where we had entered, which served as the lobby and dining room. As we sat on the bench along the large communal table, I admired the hand painted murals on the walls around me. Mahakala entered, bearing two metal bowls with pasta.

Eying the bowl in front of me, my body was ecstatic, it was about to have energy. It was my first meal since Lima. I prayed. I had been dreaming about this for days. I reached for my fork. As I went to scoop some pasta, I spotted white chunks…*Queso- Cheese?* My mind immediately went back to Cañete, the bull on the ground, blood coming from his skull, the tears running down his face- the look in his eye. *It was the first time I had been faced with this decision since my experience there on the farm. I couldn't, my gut was telling me I couldn't.*

"Mahakala, Queso?" I asked pointing at the bowl.

"Si. Si. Es queso."

Don't appear ungrateful.

"Masuru. You want more queso?"

"Yes, yes."

I scraped the chunks of queso into Masuru's bowl.

"Michael, Vegano?"

"Eh..." *I hated the label, but I didn't want to be served cheese anymore...* "Si. Pero esta bien."

I looked back at my bowl, and devoured the delicious pasta.

"Mahakala, quiero ayudar, que hace?" I asked, wanting to help and show my gratitude.

"Descanso, rest" he replied "Mañana hace pan, y Sabado vamos a la finca! Pero esta noche, descanso, descanso."

The two of us returned back up to the ashram. I hopped up in my bunk and lay there in disbelief. *Blink and you're here. Through all of the suffering - You're here with shelter and food. Here. I'm here.* I drifted off...

13 PANCITO

Day 24 December 1st

 I awoke. I was lying on the top bunk, wrapped in my sleeping bag. I looked around the room. *Cusco, you're in Cusco.* I rolled around in the bed, a huge smile across my face. *This is so comfortable. You're here.* I looked around the room from my bunk. Masuru and the 4 other strangers I shared the room with were all still fast asleep. *Go back to sleep you need rest. I can't. We've been getting up before 5 every morning. Let's explore.*

 I hopped out of bed, made my way downstairs, laced up my boots, and began walking the streets of Cusco. I landed on a corner adjacent to the San Pedro Market. There was a teenager, selling reefs to elementary school students on the corner behind me. I sat there basking in the morning sun, observing as students hurried the streets to begin their school day, dressed in their school uniforms. *We should get back and help out around the temple.*

 Wandering back to the temple, I noticed my

energy levels were extremely low. I had only walked but four blocks and my lungs could not seem to grasp enough oxygen. Walking up the hill to the temple, I felt dizzy and my body was fatigued.

As I entered back in the temple, there was a guy sitting at the large communal table behind his laptop, sporting a blonde mohawk.

"Hola amigo," I greeted the stranger.

"Hola."

My new friend Alejandro was from Venezuela, studying fashion at a university in Argentina. As we sat conversing, a girl entered. Her name was Eliana, from Bolivia. I spotted a tattoo on her wrist of kitchen utensils. She was a chef, traveling South America, experiencing and learning the cuisines of the different cultures. Masuru joined us downstairs in the main room.

"You guys come to market with me?" asked Eliana.

"Si. Claro."

"We go to get food. I cook for the temple," she explained.

The four of us made our way down to San Pedro Market to get the daily rations for the people of the temple.

Walking through the market, I watched as Eliana and Alejandro bartered with the merchants.

We ping ponged through the isles. One woman would sell us oats, another coconut flakes, another raisins. We made our way out of San Pedro, and crossed the busy street. "'The real market." Eliana informed me. Native women lined the sidewalks with fresh produce laid out in heaping piles on blankets – avocados, mangos, bananas, tomatoes, papaya, lettuce, broccoli, apples - every fruit and vegetable you could imagine.

We continued through the streets, purchasing various ingredients, making our way into another enclosed market building. It was louder, bustling with more people, more locals than San Pedro. As we squeezed through the isles, there was a strong odor that began making me nauseous. I wanted to vomit. It smelled like rotten, decaying flesh. We continued toward the end of the isle and down a few stairs. There, in front of me was half a dozen pig heads chopped from their bodies, tongues dangling from their mouth – chickens by the dozen, headless, feet still sticking off their featherless bodies. The pounds of flesh and the leaking juices gave the whole isle the smell of death.

We finished our purchases and made our way back up to the temple, bearing bags of fresh produce. On the way, we passed by a group of elementary students who were putting on an exhibit in the plaza outside the market. They were dressed in native Incan attire, explaining the history of the Incan agriculture and their staple crops: maize, quinoa, potatoes, and maca. Eliana, the chef, was fascinated and wanted to take selfies with the students in their costumes.

Arriving back at the temple, Mahakala and a few other devotees were preparing to go to the bakery to make bread.

"Michael! Michael! Buen dias. Quiere hacer pan?"

"Si. Si. Claro."

Mahakala handed me a large bucket, filled halfway with a dark, sweet smelling, transparent liquid.

"Vamos!"

We walked back down the cobblestone road, stopping at an old, unmarked wooden door. We entered through the walkway single file, to a small, enclosed courtyard and a steep sloping alleyway. At the end of the alley was another undersized wooden door. Ducking my head, we walked through a narrow, stone, corridor, which led to yet another enclosed area. To my right was a third, small wooden door. *This is something out of Alice in wonderland,* I thought to myself. I followed the gang, as we entered, again ducking as not to smash my forehead on the wall above.

We entered a windowless, stone room with a single light bulb hanging from the middle of the ceiling. To my left there was a large opening to a brick oven. The room had a very rich smell of aged wood, fresh bread, with a hint of sweetness. It was an enticing smell, making my stomach growl. The warmth coming from the oven, combined with the smell of the freshly baked bread and the dim lighting from the single bulb, gave the room a very cozy feeling. In the corner was an old radio playing music and in the center of the room stood a large wooden table covered in flour residue. Bags of flour lined the wall, and in the other corner stood the dough mixer.

The five of us removed our shirts and began making dough from scratch. Mahakala measured the flour and the wheat, adding it to the large mixing bowl. Then came the raisins and the sweet, brown sugar and linseed mixture I had carried down from the temple. The mixer cranked, and in a few minutes the dough was ready to be rolled. Equipped with a little oil and flour, we stood around the table rolling out the dough. Preparing 150 loaves or so, we covered them in towels and let them rest.

We arrived back at the temple to a magnificent meal of fruit salad, granola, vegetables, and rice, which Eliana had spent the morning preparing. After the meal, I found myself in the Temple of the temple. It was the room with an alter to Krishna - reserved for yoga, worship, and meditation. I found a book on the bookshelf that was written in English, "Life comes from Life" by A.C. Bhaktivedanta Swami Prabhupada – recorded conversations between him and a few of his disciples, discussing the essence of life and the confusions in modern science. Masuru joined me in the temple, and the two of us sat there spending the afternoon discussing faith and religion.

"Michael, Masuru," Alejandro got our attention, standing at the doorway.

"You come with Eliana and me to sell the

pan?" he asked.

"Si. Si. "

The four of us walked down to the bakery where there was a large basket filled with loaves of freshly baked bread, still warm from the oven. Alejandro reached in, grabbed a loaf, and ripped off a piece for each of us to taste.

Holy Shit.

"Muy delicioso," I said, trying to express my enjoyment.

"Si. si, muy rico," replied Alejandro.

The four of us- a Venezuelan, Bolivian, Japanese, and an American began walking up and down the streets of Cusco, together, selling bread. Out of every batch, there would be three loaves that we could use as samples to give out. For the next three hours we walked around giving out pieces of fresh bread to the people of Cusco. Once they tasted it, it was so hard not to eat more.

"Pan, Pan, Pancito!" we chanted.

"Rico Pancito!"

"Pan Pancito, con pasas y linaza!"

"Caliente, Caliente Pan! Muy fresco!"

Occasionally, we would spot very gringo looking gringos and the chant would change.

"Bread Bread! Vegan Bread! Fresh Vegan

Bread!"

The four of us explored the city, chanting, giving out bread, and meeting new people. Before we knew it, we had an empty breadbasket.

We arrived back at the temple to loud chanting and music coming from the temple room.

"Hare Krishna! Hare Krishna!"

I joined the others in the room, sitting on pillows on the wooden floor. There were drums, tambourines, triangles, and maracas. We played and chanted and played and chanted. I started working up a sweat as I shook the maracas, chanting "Hari Bol! Hari Bol!"

After the music, one of the devotees read a verse from the Bhagavad-Gita, and it was time for prasada.

About 15 of us sat around the large table in the foyer. It was Friday, and Fridays at the temple in Cusco meant pizza. As they pulled out the pizzas, covered in cheese, Mahakala handed me a bowl.

"Michael, Vegano." In the bowl were a few pieces he had made for me without cheese.

"No queso," he added, with a huge, toothy grin.

"Ah! Gracias! Gracias! Gracias!"

He sat back down, tossed me an avocado, and winked, "Queso."

I looked down at the slices of homemade pizza, covered in peppers and olives, holding the avocado I was about to smother all over them.

Am I dreaming?

14 LA FINCA

Day 25 December 2nd

"Michael! Alejandro! La Finca!" It was Mahakala.

I hopped off the top bunk, packed my bag ,and rolled my sleeping bag. Masuru was also packing. We would be going our separate ways. I said goodbye to my new hitchhiking partner and made my way down to the foyer of the temple where Mahakala, Alejandro, and a Venezuelan couple were waiting.

"Ready, Michael?"

"Si, Claro."

We all packed into a cab, which took us out of the historic area to a small bus station near downtown. Outside the bus station, a Peruvian woman had two pitchers of opaque liquids on her cart.

"Michael, quinoa or maca?"

"Bebe quinoa?" I asked, as I had never had quinoa in a beverage before.

"Si."

"Quinoa y....?"

"Manzana – apple" he replied.

"Hm.. no se."

"Quatro quinoa por favor," he addressed the lady behind the cart.

"Quinoa." I replied.

"Cinco quinoa," he told the woman.

I was handed a plastic bag filled with a warm, thick, liquid, and a neon green straw protruding from the top. *Hm...Drinking out of a plastic bag..*

I took a sip, the small balls of quinoa reminding me of boba tea as they squished in my mouth.

"Muy rico, muy dulce.. Gracias." I told Mahakala.

We entered the van and began our trek to the Sacred Valley, exiting the city, through the slums, to the farmland and the beautiful countryside of the valley.

"Michael! Michael!" Mahakala got my attention, as I stared out the window. He tossed me a giant, red, shiny bag, "Panetón" I read. It was the exact bread, the same brand that I had stared down a week prior in the truck driver's cab on the way to Arequipa.

"Come – eat," he told me.

I smiled, reached in, and ripped off a piece. It was fluffy, so fluffy and sweet.

"Muy, muy rico. Me gusta mucho. Gracias."

Everything I had dreamed of and more. Panetón!

As we drove through the valley, I looked down at the Panetón in my hand, the quinoa drink in the other, riding in a comfortable mini van that I didn't hail down from the side of the road or have to barter with. *Look outside. Look how fast were going, and you don't have to walk. Just sit, and eat and drink, you spoiled, spoiled man.*

The bus pulled off to the side of the road.

"Michael, Alejandro, la Finca!" Mahakala called out. I hopped out to see that we were in the valley, between two mountain ranges that stretched on as far as I could see, in both directions. On one side of the road was a group of buildings going up the hillside with various gardens and flowers spread about, the other side was a river and a wall of green vegetation that went up the mountainside.

Walking up to the village I was taken back by the beauty, the natural beauty – the sound of the river flowing below – the hills, lush with green grass and an abundance of flowers. Everywhere there were flowers and flowerbeds. There was even a small vegetable garden behind one of the buildings. The buildings were made of clay and glass, with solar panels on the roof. In the center stood a pavilion with hanging, bright colored hammocks.

We made our way up to the main building - a large hexagonal structure with a thatched roof, natural skylights, and large glass windows for walls. Inside the building, the floor had an intricate mosaic spreading out from the center, made from various colored tile pieces. Along the wall of windows was a long table with a bright, patterned tablecloth, about 2 feet off the ground, with cushions around it for sitting. One of the walls was opened to a large kitchen equipped with multiple stoves, sinks, and a large wooden island countertop.

As I entered, a man, his wife, and their 6-year-old daughter greeted me. They were the caretakers of the village and the farm.

I walked up the hill past the temple, to a large clay structure, a series of four dwellings. I opened one of the doors to a small room -equipped with a window, a full bed and a bunk bed, which would be my shelter for the weekend. I dropped off my bag and changed my shirt in preparation for the day's work.

Outside, I stood there observing the beauty of my surroundings. There were two llamas grazing near the temple. Hammocks hung in front of the dwellings. I could still hear the sound of the river flowing as I looked up to the surrounding mountains. *I had found another small piece of paradise.*

The crew gathered in front of the main building. It was time for work at the farm, la finca, which was located a few kilometers down the road from the village. Together, we walked down the road, running parallel to the river to la finca. A few minutes into our trek, we were reminded that it was the raining season as the clouds opened upon us with a heavy downpour.

We continued walking as water poured down from above. There was no use trying to stay dry, *just surrender*. The rain dripped from my hair down to my shirt, down to my pants, which stuck to my legs as if I had just jumped into a pool, fully clothed. We quickened the pace up the hills, off the main road as the rain turned to hail.

As we climbed up the slope, I spotted two clay dwellings with metal roofs in the distance. We booked it- running through the fields until we reached cover under the roof of the dwelling.

The floor of the half-finished building was mud, covered with straw and various pieces of wood from construction. In the corner was a very small fireplace with a metal chimney.

Cold and wet, we scoured the floor for dry pieces of wood, and started a small fire.

I rung out my shirt and watched as the water poured out before hanging it near the fire to dry. The Venezuelans pulled out a large batch of arepas and began warming them over our little fire. The five of us sat there, in a half-built clay shelter, up on the hillside, eating warm arepas and drinking kombucha, waiting for the rain to pass.

"Michael! Aqui!"

Mahakala called me over to an area on the other side of the building where a patch of the hillside had been carved out. He handed me a pickaxe and a shovel. The ground before me was separated into two layers - the top layer was clay and underneath was a mixture of stone and dirt. He pointed to two mounds under the roof of another unfinished dwelling,

"Rojo y gris," he instructed, wanting us to separate the layers of earth into two separate piles. The rojo, clay pile would be mixed with straw and water and turned into bricks for construction.

Mahakala, Alejandro, and I spent the afternoon digging into the hillside. It was a physically demanding job - yielding the pickaxe into the dense clay, shoveling the mounds of earth into buckets, and hauling bucket after bucket, each weighing at least 50 lbs.

We continued this for hours. My body and my brain began talking as my body got exhausted. *Look at yourself yielding this pickaxe. You are like one of the slaves back in Egypt, making bricks from clay. Look at the hill. You're not making a dent. A machine could clear this whole hillside in a few hours, and here you are moving it bucket by bucket.*

I started working harder, and harder trying to shut it up. *This! This is what you're doing with your life? 25 years old, digging in a hillside. They make prisoners do this shit.* Then I remembered one of the lessons from the devotee at Eco Truly. *Work, do things without attachment, freedom from outcome. Do it for the sake of doing it, and that is all. Do not glorify nor condemn it.*

We continued the work for the majority of the afternoon. There was no goal for the day, no number to hit, and no distance to get to. I began enjoying it, like a good gym session. I was sweating and covered in mud. After dumping one of the buckets I walked back to the hill,

"Fin," said Mahakala.

"That is it, Michael. We are done for the day, finished," clarified Alejandro.

My body was enthralled by the news. My shoulders, arms, legs, my entire body ached. *Better than going to the gym.*

We returned to the village.

"Prasada, Michael," Mahakala said with a smile. It was time for dinner.

Entering the hexagonal building, the communal table was set, heaping bowls of vegetables were placed at every seat. I found a seat at the table and looked out the glass windows, watching the sunset in the valley. The 8 of us sat around the table, enjoying the evening meal and each other's company.

After dinner, exhausted, I retired to my room. Day one at the farm was in the books. I lay there reflecting. *Do not praise your work, putting it up on a pedestal, and don't condemn it either. Just do it.*

December 3rd Day 26

I laid in bed, wrapped in my sleeping bag. Getting out of bed, I gazed out the small window to the green meadows covering the hillside. *You're in the sacred valley*, I reminded myself.

Finding my way down to the common building, I sat reading the Bhagavad-Gita as the farmer warmed a large pot of oatmeal over the stove. One by one, the others awoke and gathered in the building.

I looked up from my book to see oatmeal, bananas, mangos, pan, and a mango and pineapple marmalade spread out on the table. It was time for prasada.

Piece by piece, I smothered the fresh bread with the gooey, sweet marmalade. Just when I thought life couldn't get any better, the farmer busted out a big, red shiny bag of Panetón. *Oh hell yes.*

When breakfast was finished, it was time to go back to 'la finca' for the day's work. I made my way back to the farm with my amigos. We gathered our tools and attacked the mound, working in sync – shoveling, picking, loading, dumping. We filled bucket after bucket, leveling off the ground and clearing away part of the hillside. My hands, not used to wielding an axe, began to blister. My shoulder and back were still sore from the previous day. I kept going, wanting to keep the momentum of our team. We kept this up for hours, into the late afternoon, taking breaks only to sip on some homemade kombucha.

"G I Joe," joked Mahakala, as I returned from dumping a load of earth.

"Just a nice way of calling me a Gringo," I smiled.

"G I Joe – fin," he replied. We were done for the day.

Mahakala asked me if I would be staying at the farm or if I would be returning to Cusco. He informed me that everyone was returning to Cusco and I would be left at the farm alone. I enjoyed the work, but only because we had a team. I decided to return with everyone to Cusco.

We arrived back at the temple in Cusco to a large celebration. The worship room was filled with people singing, playing instruments, and chanting. After the music came a lesson from the Bhagavad-Gita and prasada.

The Sunday evening festivities came to an end, and I returned up to the Ashram where I laid on my bunk, reflecting on the day's experiences, contemplating the foundations of an Eco Village.

The sacred Valley center had been built over a span

of 10 years, using eco construction. It was built entirely by volunteers. (Pickaxe, and shovel to make bricks. Brick by brick for 10 years) It had all of these buildings, but there were no permanent residents. There was only the family that had been caring for the property for the past three months. Energy, it needed energy, human energy.

15 MAGIC

Day 27 December 4th

I awoke on the top bunk in the Ashram in Cusco - the others in the room were all still fast asleep. After morning meditation and some quick body exercises, I discovered a book near the bed "Magicians of the Gods" by Graham Hancock. I climbed back into my bunk and cracked it open.

I laid there reading, quickly getting absorbed in the theory he was proposing – a meteor crash 12,000 years ago sparking a massive increase in temperature, the melting of the ice caps, and the giant flood that destroyed ancient civilizations and their technologies. I thumbed through the pages, Cusco, Saqsaywaman – ruins left by a "Pre-Incan" civilization with building technologies far superior than that of the Incas. I was fascinated.

"Michael! Alejandro!" It was Eliana.

"You will come with me to the market?" she asked in her Bolivian accent, smiling, as she stood at the doorway. Girls were not allowed in the Ashram de Devotees.

"Si! Si, Vamos!" I answered closing the book and hopping off my bunk.

Instead of going directly to the market, we took an alternate route, climbing a flight of stairs that overlooked the city. My new friends sparked a morning joint to start the day. *Damn. That smell reminds me of LA, the 1 bedroom apartment, smoking joints in the living room with Adam as we worked on our stoner movie.*

"Michael, Quieres?"

"No, Gracias" *I had no interest in smoking but the smell, man, I loved the smell.*

The three of us walked down to the market bringing bags and soles to purchase food for the devotees and volunteers that day.

The market was busy as usual.

"Papi! Papi! ! Un sole! Un sole!" The women tried getting my attention waving fresh tomatoes and mangos in my face.

"Mami! Mami!" They fought for Eliana's attention, "Dos soles Mami. Dos soles!" pointing at avocados, papaya, and pineapple.

Zig-zagging through the market, the soles were gone, and we had two large bags filled with fresh fruit and vegetables for the day. With about 45 soles (roughly 14USD), and Eliana's bartering skills, we were able to get enough food for about 12-15 people to have two meals.

At the temple we began preparing the food for the first meal. Mahakala had slept in, meaning we would not be preparing bread that day. I took the position as Eliana's su chef, washing peeling, and chopping fruit for the fruit salad.

After lunch, I made my way to the Ashram to return to Graham Hancock's theories about Cusco. I noticed as I lay there, I was getting comfortable...too comfortable. *If you're here, you're either learning something, or you're teaching something without you knowing it.* I prayed. *Please make the next lesson clear.*

"Michael!" It was Mahakala, *I must have dozed off reading.*

"Quieres va a la mercado?" asking if I wanted to go to the market.

Was it the next day already? Did I sleep through dinner?

"Que? La Mercado?"

"Si. Con los Devotees. Musica en la Mercado."

"Musica? Si, bueno."

I hopped off the bunk, threw on my boots and barrowed a jacket from Alejandro. There was a large group of about ten people waiting in the lobby with instruments and bags to bring down to the market. We entered San Pedro. As a group we played instruments - drums, tambourine, bells, and chanted,

"Hari Bol! Hari Bol! Hari Bol! Hare Krishna! Hare Krishna! Krishna, Krishna!"

I followed, chanting along, as merchants began unloading pounds of produce into my open bag. We walked up and down the isles, chanting, playing instruments, and filling one basket after another with donated food - bananas, avocados, rice, corn, broccoli, tomatoes, and peppers. After about 40 minutes we had too much food to carry through the streets.

I posted up outside of the San Pedro market with about 7 full bags of produce as the group continued over to the market across the street. They returned about a half hour later with another 7 or so overflowing bags.

I stood there on the curb, outside the San Pedro Market surrounded by bags and bags of fresh produce. *0 soles,* I thought to myself, *0 soles*. I remembered my prayer that afternoon. *That morning we had gone to the market with 45 soles and we brought bag 2 bags. Tonight, we went down with instruments and praise and brought back over 14. It was a miracle. No necesito soles.* A devotee hailed a cab, and we loaded the bounty up to be hauled to the temple.

As, we sat around the table eating dinner, a guy entered carrying his bags.

"Thor! Thor!" the people around me at the

table cheered.

"Nice jacket," he said to me as I sat there, looking down at the jacket.

Ahh this is his. Alejandro gave me his jacket to borrow.

Samuel, also known as Thor, for his long hair, had just returned from a trip to Machu Picchu. After dinner, we went up to the Ashram and I discovered that Magicians of the Gods belonged to him as well. As we sat there discussing the theories of Graham Hancock, the conversation transitioned over to life philosophies, hallucinogens, and everything under the sun. *This guy is like a long lost brother*, I thought to myself.

16 SIMPLE LIFE

Day 28-31: December 5th-8th Temple at Cusco

Over the next few days I fell in love with the city of Cusco and each part of my day. The mornings were spent at the market and baking fresh bread. The afternoons were for eating, worshiping, and resting. At night I would roam the city selling bread and chanting,

"Pan! Pan! Pancito! Muy rico, Pancito!" as I met different travelers from all over the world and made friends with the local merchants. I would return to a vegetarian dinner – pizza, empanadas, eggplant, all prepared fresh. It was all very grand, except I noticed myself falling into a routine, becoming comfortable. Also, during this time, I got a second round of traveling sickness and my weight began to drop, as my body was not able to absorb nutrients from the food. The Italians, two new volunteers, were also having the same issue. We concluded it was the water – no more tea, no more kombucha – no more soup.

December 9th Day 32

Ah shit. My stomach is killing me. Let's go. We gotta get to the bathroom. I rushed to the bathroom. *Damn. Someone is showering.* I ran down the stairs to the 1st floor bathroom – open. *Thank God.*

As I exited, I heard a knock on the temple door. I opened the door to be greeted by the ultimate Rasta–yogi-traveler, sporting boots, a massive pack, dreadlocks, and a sweet looking farmer's hat slung over his pack. I greeted him,

"Hola Amigo, Cómo estás?"

"Bien. Es de templo de Hare Krishna?" he asked with a bit of an accent.

"Si. Si,"

"Hable Inglés?"

"Yeah, I'm from California."

"Ah dude, thank God. Same. What's up?"

"I met a Hare Krishna at San Pedro yesterday, he sold me some bread. We started chatting and he said I could volunteer at la finca today. He said to be here by 8."

"Ah dope. Yeah I'm just packing my bag, we should be leaving in a few. Just hang out. It's gonna be me you and a third guy, Samuel."

I ran upstairs to grab my bag. The three of us

left the temple, heading to the Sacred Valley. We made a quick pit stop at San Pedro- my friends wanted some juice before heading to the bus station.

As we sipped carrot and banana juice, I learned about our new Rasta friend, Jacob. He had spent 2 years backpacking South America, and he now worked on a Marijuana farm up in Northern California. After Cusco, he was planning to visit an Eco Village in Chile to spend a few weeks there.

We left the market, took a cab to the bus stop, and a bus up to la finca. Exiting the bus, I found myself again, surrounded by mountains, the river, and gardens, deep in the Sacred Valley. We made our way up to the main building bearing gifts of pan and Panetón. The first to greet me was the little girl. She ran over to me gave me a hug and began counting in English, her little way of showing off.

"1,2,3,4,5,6,7,8,9,10,11,12,14"

"No, no, no.. 13..14"

"10,11,12,…14,15.."

"No. 10,11,12,13! 14.."

"..11,12..13,14,…."

"Bueno!"

"…20!" She yelled as she ran away.

We dropped our gifts off at the kitchen and prepared for work. The Venezuelan couple from the previous weekend was now living at la finca. The five of us began our trek from the village to la finca. There I was back in the Sacred Valley at the farm, pickaxe, in hand, with a new squad, Samuel, Jacob, and the Venezuelan. We had a blast, working on the hillside together.

"Crossfit," joked the Venezuelan as we picked, shoveled, and hauled the earth. Together we transformed the hill into two piles of clay and earth, leveling off the ground.

The farmer came around to inspect, "Fin."

Trekking back to the village, we took an alternate route through the mountainside. As we hiked, Jacob randomly stopped on the trail and sniffed the air like a dog.

"Smell that?" he asked as he sniffed the leaves of the plants in the surrounding area. Analyzing them, sniffing more, me smiled and picked a patch of leaves. It was a special herb for tea, he informed me. As we continued back, this sniffing occurrence continued to repeat itself. I didn't pay much attention. I was too mesmerized by the massive air plants, clinging to the face of the cliff which bordered the path.

The village came into view just as the clouds began to remind us that it was the raining season. We quickened the pace, making a beeline to the shelter as the rain continued to get heavier. We ran, arriving just as the rain turned to hail. I sat there staring out the large, glass windows into the valley, observing the beautiful storm. Sheltered, tired, thankful, I sat reading the Bhagavad-Gita before dinner was served. After dinner, I went right to bed.

December 10th Day 33

I hopped out of bed feeling sore, but fully energized from the 10 hours of sleep. I packed my bag and made my way to the temple for meditation. Shortly after, Madre came in to the temple to perform a ceremony with incense, flowers, perfumes, and the ringing of a bell. She was "awakening the deity" as I learned in Eco Truly. As she was finishing the ceremony, Samuel, Jacob, the farmer, his daughter, and the Venezuelans, joined us. Together, we spent the next hour playing instruments and chanting.

Before breakfast, I helped the farmer in the small garden behind his house, digging a few rows, planting pink and yellow flowers. It was time for breakfast - bread, mangos, bananas. I sat and observed mostly during the meals at the farm. Everyone spoke fluid Spanish. I would listen and try to figure out the main points, but sometimes I would just tune everyone out.

I followed the farmer up the hill past the house, behind the temple to the llama pen. He pointed at a nearby wheelbarrow, handed me a shovel. "Llama poop, por la finca," he said with a smile. Jacob followed us up to the pen and began raking the piles as I fetched the wheelbarrow.

"This is some really good shit man," he told me as he reached down and picked up some dried pellets with his hand, "Really good shit…Mix this with alfalfa." Together, we finished cleaning the pen, and had a heaping wheelbarrow full of llama droppings. I smiled, just watching him awe over the pile of manure.

"I know its kind of crazy how excited I'm getting over some llama shit, but this will grow you some good crops."

We took turns hauling the wheelbarrow of droppings from the village to la finca. I spent the first part of the afternoon fertilizing a small garden area with dried cow manure, breaking up the large chunks with my hands and spreading it out over the ground. The second part of the afternoon was spent building a gutter system with Jacob.

Jacob and I were instructed to hang a gutter on the side of the half built, clay shell. Tampering, jimmy rigging, and using the limited hand tools we had, we attempted to secure the gutter to the roof. It was a job that would have taken about an hour with the proper power tools.

By the end of the afternoon, it was secured and a large plastic drum was placed under the spout. Water could now be collected to make bricks, and construction could continue. Our job for the day was done.

Back at the yoga village, I was on my way to

the main building to rest before the return trip to Cusco.

"Michael, I wanted to give you these," Jacob stopped me on my walk, handing me a plastic bag filled with, what appeared to be dehydrated beans.

"You have a long journey ahead of you back to Lima. They are Ica nuts, Peruvian nuts, very dense, high fat – perfect fuel for traveling."

"Gracias Amigo." I hugged my new friend. *This wasn't just a bag of nuts - I now had fuel for the return trip to Lima.*

I knew this was my last day in the Sacred Valley. I said goodbye to my friends at the farm, the farmers wife, the Venezuelans, Jacob, their daughter – picking her up as she counted for me in English. Goodbye llamas, Goodbye Mountains, Goodbye River. Goodbye Finca.

Samuel, the farmer, and I went down to the road to catch a bus back into Cusco. We arrived at the temple to Sunday festivities- dancing, singing, and music, and a lesson from the Bhagavad-Gita – Chapter 18 verse 42.

"Tranquility, restraint, austerity, purity, patience, integrity, knowledge, wisdom and firm faith – these are the qualities of work for the Brahmins."

17 "COINCIDENCE"

Day 34 December 11th

Waking at the temple back in Cusco, I resumed the routine. Mahakala had slept in, meaning we would not be selling bread today.

With a free afternoon, I grabbed the book "Life comes from Life" and made my way down to the plazas to find a nice place to sit and read. Walking down near the Plaza de Armor, I began looking for an open bench when I heard someone call my name. I turned to see a white male, about my age, sitting on one of the benches. He looked strangely familiar.

"Michael! Wow! You made it to Cusco!"

Seeing that I was still trying to place his face, he continued,

"It's Colby. Colby from Lima."

"Ah!" *the kids from the park bench in Mira Flores...* "Yes! Yes! How are you?"

"Holy shit! It's you. I can't believe I ran into you. We've been talking about you since you left, wondering if we would somehow run into you again or if you would even make it here."

"I'm here, made it," I smiled thinking back to the journey.

"How did you get here? Wait. Dude. Where are you staying? We have an extra room at our hostel, it's pretty sick. You can crash with us."

"Ah thanks man. I'm staying up at the Hare Krishna Temple near San Pedro."

"You gotta come see Bryce, he's not gonna believe I ran into you."

We walked through the streets, chatting and catching up, making our way back to their apartment.

On our walk, we bumped into Bryce who was hanging outside a laundry mat waiting for his clothes to finish.

"Holy Shit. Look who it is. How did you find him?" he asked Colby.

"Just sitting in the Plaza De Armor, and I was like.. is that him? Is that the same guy?"

"Yeah man, you look different. Looks like you've lost a ton of weight," added Bryce.

"Ha yeah. Just a little bit" - between the traveling sickness and 5 days of nearly fasting, I was beginning to swim in my clothes.

"Well you're alive. That's great."

I laughed. "It's been a wild ride."

"You gotta tell."

I left off from the last time we saw each other and told them of my journey and adventures as we walked the streets of Cusco.

"Water?" asked Bryce pointing to a large gallon of bottled water as we arrived at the apartment.

"Yes. That would be awesome." I hadn't been drinking anything at the temple due to the traveling sickness, getting my hydration through fruit at lunch.

As I continued with the story, relaying to them the experience of freezing up in the mountains of Espinar – Bryce disappeared from the kitchen, returning a few moments later holding a sweater.

"Here, You have to take this. It's warm. A gift. Please. For your trip home."

I stared at the blue and white knitted sweater. It had a hood and a zipper that went down the front. "Hand made here in Cusco," he said, smiling.

I embraced my friend "Thank you. This is awesome. Thank you."

We spent the next few hours sitting at the table in the kitchen of their apartment. We discussed eco construction, capitalism, travel, and our dreams for the future, even Graham Hancock's ancient civilization theories. They were both huge fans of Joe Rogan's podcast and had listened to his interview with Hancock. The two of them began telling me about Saqsaywaman – the archeological site mentioned in Hancock's book. They informed me that it was just a short hike up the mountain from the plaza, near the large statue of Jesus that over looked the city. *It keeps following me. You have to visit.*

"Do you need tickets?" I asked.

"Yeah. It costs money to get in. "

"Ah, oh well, maybe another trip."

It was beginning to get late and my friends had plans for their last night in Cusco. They were grabbing drinks with two girls from Ireland. Together we walked back to the plaza and said our goodbyes.

18 INSTINCT

Day 35- 36 December 12th-13th

    I could feel that my time at the temple was coming to an end. My flight to Dallas was booked for the 20th. It had taken me 5 days to get from Eco Truly to Cusco, traveling (hitching, walking, driving) at least 19hrs per day. For the return trip, I had to be strategic. I knew that without a hitch, it was about a three-weeks journey by foot. If I got a hitch right from Cusco to Lima – I could be there in 2 days like the tour buses. There was a large variable of 19 days. I knew that once I left the temple, once I walked out that front door in Cusco– there was no more guarantee of food, water, or shelter until I reached my sisters apartment in Dallas, Texas. Every day I stayed at the temple, I had food and a place to sleep, but I was cutting it closer with my flight, becoming more and more dependant on a swift hitch. The thought of being back out in the cold with no shelter, without food, or water weighed heavy on my mind. At the time my body was still battling the travelers sickness, and my energy levels were extremely low.

I told Mahakala that tomorrow, Thursday, would be my last day at the temple. I would be beginning my trek back to Lima before anyone awoke Friday morning.

19 MORE MAGIC

Day 37 December 14th – Last day in Cusco

I awoke on a mat on the floor, staring up at the ceiling, looking at the walls – I would be saying goodbye. I felt this strong urge to visit Saqsaywaman. *It's your last day. Enjoy it.*

"Michael, my Michael," it was Eliana's voice coming from the hallway.

"You come to the market?"

"Si. Si. Vamos!"

Goodbye market – the colors, the sounds, the smells, the bright reds of the tomatoes, brown and yellows of the bundles of bananas, the rows of green, leafy vegetables, the chanting, "Un Sole! Papi! Mami! Limon! Mango! Chala!" the souring smell of aged cheese as it warmed in the sun.

I carried the bags of produce back up to the temple, and made one last fruit salad with Eliana.

After lunch I laid on my mat reflecting on my time there at the temple, ready for the next step of the journey.

"Michael, Vender Pan?" It was Alejandro.

"Si, claro."

With a basket full of warm bread, we made our way through the streets,

"Pan, pan! Pancito con pasas y linaza!"

The day was zipping by. The sun was setting and about 5 loaves remained as I looked up the hillside, spotting the statue of Jesus.

"Alejandro, you want to go to Saqsaywaman?"

"No." He replied with a smile.

"Come on. We go and sell pan along the way."

"No, no. It is far. You go. I finish."

"Dude, come on."

"No, I go back to temple. You go."

I handed him the basket, making my way up the street in the direction of the statue. The sun had almost completely set. It was getting dark, and I wanted to be sure I was taking the correct route. A few blocks up the hill, I stopped at a shop.

"Saksecuyumuyan?" I asked, pointing up the hill.

"Que?"

"Sakeseywymon? The ruins? El ruins?" I tried explaining.

The man laughed.

"Ah. Sexy Waman. You go sexy woman?"

"No. No. El artifacto, by statue of Jesus."

"Si. Si. Saxy-wamon. Saqsay-waman."

"Si. Si. Up the hill?"

"Yes. But it is closed. It is night time."

"How far?"

"Ehh.. 30-40 minute walk, but it is closed. It is dark. It is dangerous.

"It's ok."

"There are no lights on the path. It is up the cliffs, very dangerous. Go tomorrow during the day."

"Gracias."

I began walking back down the road, in the direction of the temple. When I reached the bottom of the hill I stopped.

What are you scared of?

I turned around and begin trekking back up the hill, past the shop, up until the road ended and turned into a narrow stairway. I continued climbing up the hillside through narrow passages and dark staircases. I hiked the stone pathways and stairs, up, up, up, until I reached a gate, with a sign hanging above,

"Parque Arqueologico De Saqsaywaman." To the left of the gate was a ticket booth with the light on, but no one was inside. Another sign hung stating that the park was closed, yet the gate was open.

Lit by the moonlight, I continued my trek up the cobblestone path, though the gate. There was a cliff on my right. I could not see down for it was too dark, however I could hear the sound of flowing water, a stream. I continued up, and up the path.

Summiting the hill, there to my left, stood a magnificent wall, constructed of boulders, magnificent, enormous masses of stone stuck snugly together with perfect seems. As I neared, I could feel their energy, the vibration. It was weird, as if part of me was drawn to the stones – I opened my arms and pressed my body against them, absorbing the vibrations. I felt like I had been transported to a different world, like that of Alice in Wonderland or a human living in a world of giants.

I continued up the path, along the wall, coming to an entrance, with stairs leading up through the wall to more ruins. A rope went across the entrance to the staircase with a sign "No entrar."

Hopping over the rope, I climbed up the staircase, into the ruins. Lit by the moonlight, I walked around, observing the structures, making my way up a hill to the foundation of a building. There I was, climbing through the massive ruins of this ancient city, alone, under the moonlight. No tour guide – no security officers – no boundaries - free to explore. I climbed up onto one of the massive, finely crafted boulders, and sat overlooking the lights of the city of Cusco below. It was a magical feeling, being alone among the ancient ruins.

Thank you Cusco. Thank you.

Returning to the temple, I passed Mahakala along the way, posted up in front of the yoga shop near San Pedro, selling pan.

"Michael! I go deliver kombucha. Come." Carrying 2 bottles of homemade kombucha, we walked the streets of Cusco as I practiced my Spanish with Mahakala. I found myself back on the same road where I started my trek to Saqsaywaman. Across the street from where the man told me to go home was the tattoo parlor where we delivered the bottles of kombucha.

"I want to show you other temple, es Vegan restaurante. Vive aqui en temple por cinco años," Mahakala told me.

We walked a few blocks up the hill and entered the vegan restaurant.

"Vegan burger?" Asked Mahakala.

"Si. Claro!" I had cheffed up quite a few vegan burgers back in LA and was curious to see if the Peruvians knew what they were doing.

We sat in the kitchen as the chef prepared two vegan burgers topped with chutney, hummus, red peppers, and guacamole. *So bomb.*

There was a girl from Sweden who was volunteering at the temple. The three of us had a great conversation discussing books, philosophy, and again, the Alchemist.

We returned to the temple, and I made my way upstairs to make sure everything was in order for my departure in a few hours. As I reached the top of the stairs, my friends, Eliana, Alejandro, Samuel and the Italian couple were all standing outside the Ashram. They began singing "happy traveling to you" to the tune of Happy Birthday, and gifted me a bag of fruit and nuts. *Thank you. Thank you. Thank you! I was blessed.* I had come to the temple with four apples and they multiplied into bananas, nuts, mangos, and dried fruit. *Energy is not created or destroyed it is transferred.*

I said goodbye and goodnight to all of my new friends in Cusco. I crawled in my sleeping bag, and asked the Italian who was sleeping on the bunk near my mat to set an alarm for 4:30. I laid there in my sleeping bag with my map out, debating the best route back to Lima. Again, I faced two options.

Option 1: Cutting West through the mountains to Abancay and Puquio over to Nazca. It was the reverse path I had attempted to take with

Masuru before we retreated back to Nazca.

Pros: Shorter distance. *New road I hadn't traveled before.*

Cons: Mountain climate, high altitude, freezing temperatures, extremely dangerous roads, not a lot of traffic.

Option 2: Taking the long route South, down to Arequipa and back up the coast to Nazca.

Pros: High traffic roads, a lot of trucks from Arequipa to Lima, warm temperatures, I could sleep outside if I had to.

Cons: Longer distance. *I had already traveled those roads*

To the mountains we go.

20 HITCHY-HIKEY

Day 38 December 15th

Alarm buzzing I awoke on the floor of the Ashram.

Turn off the alarm. I'm still tired. Just a few more minutes of sleep, please, I'm so comfortable.

No.

I got my body to sit up.

It's still dark outside. Come on, lay down, just sleep a little longer.

No.

Come on. Your flight isn't for 6 more days. One more day at the temple won't hurt. Just one more day. You can leave tomorrow.

No.

I crawled out of my bag and began rolling it up.

What about breakfast, at least stay for breakfast, one more meal at the temple?

No. Stop. We're leaving.

I grabbed my bag and walked out the front door of the temple. It was almost 5, the magic hour for hitching. Standing there on the sidewalk, I thought to myself, *you have to find the main road to Abancay. You have to get out of Cusco. Remember, large cities are like magnets, all of the traffic is coming in. It has a strong pull. It took you two days to get out of Lima.*

As I stood there, contemplating the best direction to walk, a cab driver pulled along side of me and rolled down his window.

"Me amigo, donde es la pista a Abancay? No necesito ride. Just directions," I asked the man for directions to Abancay in my best Spanglish. He thought for a few moments, and then pointed up the hill behind him.

"Gracias," I told the stranger.

He reached over, unlocked the door signaling me to get in.

"Ah, no. No Gracias. Yo caminar. No tengo soles. Me gusta caminar," I said smiling.

"No. No. It's very close. Hop in. I take you. Esta bien. Esta bien," he waved me into his cab.

In the cab, we weaved in and out of a few alleys, up a hill, down to a highway, up another hill, and a few minutes later he stopped the car at an intersection.

"Aqui. Road to Abancay," he pointed up and down the road.

"Muchas, muchas Gracias."

I reached into the gift bag from my friends and handed the driver two bananas.

"Gracias, amigo."

"Ah! Muchas Gracias"

I stood there on the side of the road, observing the traffic, planning my next move. There were a lot of local buses, mini vans, and cabs, people heading off to work. Not much truck traffic. *I hope this is the right road. I hope this is the right road.*

I walked over to a group of locals waiting for the bus,

"Abancay?"

"Ah, Si. Si, Abancay."

"Bueno."

I threw my thumb up. Occasionally, a large tractor-trailer would come barreling down the road. My hitching attempts were not working out.

"… patience, integrity, knowledge, wisdom.."

An old, beat up, pick-up truck pulled off to the side of the road.

"Donde Va?" The man asked.

"Abancay.. y tu donde?"

"25 km mas."

"…a Abancay?"

"Si, si."

"Bueno! Gracias!"

There was a man in the passenger seat. I climbed in the back.

Cruising down the road toward Abancay, I looked out over Cusco. *Goodbye Cusco. Goodbye temple. Goodbye.*

We reached the town of Ante, and my new amigos pulled over. Knowing this was the end of the road, I reached in my bag and gave them bananas and mangos. "Gracias," I hopped out.

Ante was a small town with few small shops along the main road and a single gas station. I began walking down the road, enjoying the feeling of making progress, and moving in the right direction. I tried hitching every vehicle that passed that wasn't marked as a cab. A few trucks blew by me. Minutes started passing and my momentum began to dwindle. *You'll catch one. Relax. It's early.*

Standing there across from the gas station, a pick-up pulled off to the side of the road in front of me. It looked like one of the government owned security- pickups, the same one that had rescued me from the cliffs of Espinar.

I ran up to the side of the vehicle, not wanting to get my hopes up.

"Donde Va?" the man asked me.

"Abancay."

"Abancay? Come on! Vamos!" he invited me in.

I closed the door behind me, *Look at you man, look at you – you're flying. You'll be in Abancay before noon.*

There was a dense fog blocking the view as we drove up the winding road, playing top 40 American hits over the radio. We jammed out in his car singing and conversing in Spanglish with each other. He was bragging about Peru and their produce. He stopped and bought me an avocado from a woman on the side of the road.

The driver, Edwin, was 35 and lived in an apartment in Cusco. He worked as an engineer and loved his beer and fútbol. We reached Abancay around 11, and he drove me to the road that continued to Lima. He dropped me on a corner and pointed down the road, "Nazca, Lima."

The road was narrow and led through the town. I stood there observing. *There is no way an 18-wheel tractor-trailer can fit down this road- this can't be the right road. I need a highway, man- a highway with some trucks.*

The traffic was mostly cabs. I asked a woman

standing next to me on the sidewalk waiting for a cab,

"Hola, es la pista de Lima?"

"Si," she responded, pointing in the same direction as Edwin.

"Gracias."

Then a large tractor-trailer came driving down the road. I watched, as he got closer continuing towards me, the traffic going in the opposite direction had to pull off to the side as he squeezed through the narrow street. I waved, and waved trying to get his attention.

"Lima! Lima!"

He shook his head and continued driving.

Another half hour or so passed before the next truck came down the road.

"Lima, Lima, Nazca!" I chanted, smiling, waving my thumb in the air.

This time, the driver signaled that he had just arrived in Abancay. This was his destination.

I could feel the adrenaline of my morning travel starting to wear off. *High energy. High energy. Come on.*

I stood there on the side of the road about 2 hours from Cusco and 20 hours from Lima. Something about being alone, standing on a sidewalk in a completely unfamiliar town, in a foreign country, with no money, knowing that I have no where to sleep and no where to go is simultaneously the most depressing and exhilarating feeling I have experienced.

My brain wanted to go into safety mode. *It's clearly not a tourist town. You are the only gringo. I wonder how they feel about gringos here. If you don't catch a ride, you'll be sleeping here. Find a backup place to sleep, a gas station, start scouting.*

No, we don't need a place to sleep. It's noon. We need a better place to hitch.

I walked down the road until I came to a fork. There was a sign "Lima" pointing down and to the right.

Yes, hope.

A truck was approaching from behind. I stood there across from the sign with my thumb up smiling, waving my arm to get his attention. *Come on, baby. Come on.* He looked at me. Then shook his head smiling.

A few cars behind, another truck, nearly identical to the one that had just passed came down the road.

"Lima! Lima! Nazca! Lima!" I chanted with my thumb high in the air.

The truck stopped in the middle of the road,

holding up the traffic behind him. I yelled up to the cab to be heard over the loud engine,

"Nazca! Nazca! Lima!"

The door opened, the driver patted the seat next to him. I climbed up into the truck.

"Gracias, amigo. Donde va?" I asked the man who was sporting a tight, sweat stained, turquoise t-shirt, navy construction pants, and flip-flops.

"Puquio! Puquio!" he chanted.

"Puquio. Perfecto."

"Si. Si. Puquio… Mañana, Nazca y Lima."

I smiled. I laughed.

"No way! No! No way!" I couldn't contain my joy.

"Va a Lima? Mañana?" I asked, wanting to make sure I heard him correctly.

"Si. Si." He smiled at my excitement, "Lima es mi destonacion final."

"Voy con tu a Lima?" I asked.

"Si. Si. Lima! Lima! Lima!" He chanted.

"Lima! Lima!" I joined.

I settled back into the seat.

You did it. You did it, man. -I had caught a big one, the

perfect hitch. Shelter for the next 20 hours - Is this real?

Tomorrow night you'll be back in Lima…. Then what?

Stop. Stop. A moment ago you were eyeing a sidewalk to crash on in Abancay. Stop thinking 5 steps ahead. This is a gift. Enjoy this moment. Enjoy this ride.

The driver, Jenier, was 28. He was a Lima native who lived in an apartment with his new wife of 3 months. The two of us cruised down the road. Next stop, Puquio.

We spent the next 11 hours driving through the mountains of Peru, headed west. We were following his compañero, the man who passed me in the identical truck. They both worked for the same company and drove together, one following the other like a team. As we drove, we sang, talked, and shared stories. His English was about as good as my Spanish. He would play an American song, and I would translate it best I could into Spanish. Then we would switch. We snacked on the fruit, bread and nuts that I had from the temple as we drove through snow-capped mountains. *Hell of a road trip.*

We arrived in the town of Puquio around 11PM. Puquio, a mountain town at high altitude, had a pretty low temperature and strong winds. We drove through the town and stopped at a small truck stop with a restaurant, up in the mountains. Jenier and his compañero wanted dinner.

As we crossed the street to the restaurant, I noticed a church building next door. It had a front porch with a wall made of stone for a railing. *You can put your sleeping bag down on the porch right near the wall and be sheltered from the wind. It's a church. No one will mess with you.*

They ordered pan y huevos and pan y queso and Jenier got me some tea.

"Michael, do you have tent?"

"No, pero esta bien. I have sleeping bag."

"Where you will sleep tonight?"

"Maybe next door, on the porch of the church."

He smiled. "Sleep in back of my truck."

"Si?"

"Si."

After they finished their food, we went back out to the trucks. I grabbed my sleeping bag from the front cabin as Jenier unlocked the hatch to the Cargo. I climbed up into the back of the cargo container. It was pitch black, almost completely sealed- the sound of the wind blew through the cracks. It smelled like fresh cut wood. It was cold, ice cold. I felt around with my hands – sawdust, lumber, stacks of freshly cut lumber. I continued feeling around in the dark. The pile was a little over waste high and continued all across the width of the container. I hopped up with my sleeping bag, took off my boots, unrolled the bag, and slid in. There on that pile of lumber, covered in sawdust, in the back of the tractor-trailer, in the mountains of

Puquio, I drifted off to sleep. I was awoken by the sound of barking dogs outside the truck - relentless barking. My feet were cold, freezing. I tried warming them with my hands and rubbing my toes together, eventually I drifted back off to sleep.

December 16th

Day 39 AM

I awoke as the truck engine fired up, "Michael! Michael! Vamos!" I heard Jenier call from outside the hauling container.

I hopped off the pile of lumber, put my shoes on, grabbed my sleeping bag, and was greeted by Jenier as I slid back the door.

"Let's go. Let's go," eager to hit the road.

I hopped down shook out my sleeping bag – *Oh no! No! My stomach.* The sickness was back.

"Jenier. Un momento." I ran over to a nearby port-a-potty. Occupado. *What?! No. No way. No way! It's 3:30 in the morning in the mountains of Puquio! Someone else is in here right now?*

I stood there my stomach squirming. The door opened and a man exited. *Finally.*

A few minutes later I was back sitting shotgun and we were en route to Nazca for desayuno, breakfast.

That morning we drove through the small town where Masuru and I had retreated, up in the mountains. *I can't believe I went to Cusco and came back again, already.* We drove down the winding roads, down past the woman on the side of the road- still selling her sweets and cola to the truck drivers at the weigh station, back into the town of Nazca.

Jenier pulled off to the side of the road as we entered the town - right across the street from where I stood for hours, trying to hitch a ride to Cusco. I was back. Jenier and his compañero wanted breakfast. We walked over to the small market in the median of the two main roads. Jenier insisted that he buy me breakfast.

"Me amigo, gracias, pero estoy bien."

"No. No. Tu comes!"

"No come huevos, carne, y queso. Estoy bien. Gracias." I explained.

"Que! No come huevos y queso!" he and his buddy laughed.

"Si. Si."

"Aqui, come. Pan y vegetable tortilla," he handed me a roll, inside was a folded tortilla with chunks of vegetables.

"Quinoa or maca?" he asked.

"Quinoa," I replied with a large grin, I knew what I was doing this time.

I enjoyed the hot quinoa beverage and ate my pan.

It was time to hit the road again.

We drove, and we drove, and we drove. We reached Ica, driving down the Pan-American south. I stared out the window laughing at how far I had walked in the wrong direction when I had first arrived in Ica. It was a 15-minute drive from the town center to the car lot where I finally realized I was walking in the wrong direction. *What an idiot.*

Passing through Ica, I knew we were getting close. A few hours later, I saw a sign for Cañete. We were getting closer and closer. *Hey man, we are almost in Lima. What are you gonna do then, huh?*

It was dark out about 8pm when we reached the city limits. We had done it.

"Mi amigo, Lima!" Jenier celebrated.

"Si! Si! Lima!" I tried to sound enthusiastic but my brain had already begun overloading with questions. *Where do you hop out? Where are you going to go tonight? Where are we going to sleep?*

"Mi amigo. Donde va?"

"Uhh… No se."

"No se?"

"No. It doesn't matter. Anywhere you want to stop is fine. I'll hop out."

"Que? Donde?"

"No es importante. Aqui, Allí, Lima, Mira Flores. No es importante."

"You go to Mira Flores?"

"Uhh.. Si. Mira Flores."

I rode back with Jenier to the station where he and his compañero parked their trucks and their cargo. He had just driven me over 559 miles.

"Mi amigo. Gracias." I gifted Jenier the remaining fruit from my friends in Cusco. He gave me a hug, Muchas gracias.

Leaving the truck lot, my friends got a cab and told me to hop in.

"We go north. Tell you when to hop out," Jenier informed me.

We were inland, east of Lima. Together we went west out to the main highway. He pulled off to the shoulder of the highway under an overpass. I recognized the area. I spotted the massive shopping mall where I had watched the couple play chess and saw the Star Wars exhibit, and I was on the opposite side of highway from where I caught the first van to Cañete.

"Aqui. Here. Adios. Goodbye my friend."

"Gracias! Muchas gracias! Thank you!"

I watched the cab, carrying my new friends, disappear down the highway.

There I was, back in Lima, standing on the side of the highway. I had an avocado, a bag of Ica nuts, and 4 days until my flight. *What's your plan, man? Mira Flores, go find a place to sleep in Mira Flores.*

As I walked back to the coast, I kept experiencing drastic mood swings and shifts in energy. One moment everything was perfect. *I was alive. I had made it 40 days. I just had an awesome hitch from Cusco. I was OK. The next moment it switched… I had no money, no place to sleep. I was hungry, but worse… I was alone.*

I began examining parking garages and the alleys between houses, looking for a place to put my sleeping bag for the night. *Dude, this is sketchy, the valet drivers keep shooting you dirty looks every time you get near a garage. Well, let's go over your options…You either find a safe place to put your sleeping bag or you ask a stranger to sleep on their floor…*

On a side street bordering Mira Flores, a man exited his apartment building to walk his dog. *He looks friendly - he's got a dog. You've got nothing to lose.* I approached the man,

"Hola Mi amigo. Necesito un place a dormir esta noche… puedo dormir a su casa? Tengo un sleeping bag. Solo necesito un floor," I explained in Spanglish pointing at my sleeping bag. Not completely understanding my question, the man began directing me to a hostel in a very polite, calm, and friendly manner.

I interrupted the man,

"No mi amigo, No entiendes. Tengo 0 soles.
No usar Hostel. Puedo dormir a su casa? SU casa?"

The man paused, staring at me. I could se his brain
speeding up as he began to make sense of my
request. He began shaking his head as it clicked –
HIS house I wanted to stay at HIS house.

"Oh no. No. No, no mi casa!" he looked at me
in disgust, as if I had deeply offended him. He
turned around and yanked his dog as he began
walking swiftly away from me.

Well...That went well.

I continued my trek into Mira Flores, the
streets now starting to look familiar. An idea
popped in my head. *The park - the park with the
flowers near the beach, maybe you can sleep there.*

I made it to the park, the beautiful park on the
cliffs, overlooking the Pacific Ocean. I walked
around, checking near walls, bushes, trees,
continuing to scout for a spot to sleep – *too much
light – security/cops will definitely kick me out – Where
can you hide out…*

I spotted two guys working out on a set of bars
nearby. *Make friends maybe they'll offer to let you crash
on their floor.*

"Hola Amigos, Cómo estás?"

I spent the next hour hanging out with two
guys who had just left an all you can eat sushi place
and were trying to work it off before going to bed.
One was a surfer and the other a personal trainer.

They kept working out, but I could no longer hang. I was exhausted. My body was still suffering from traveler's sickness, and I was running on the three hours of sleep I had in Puquio. *I just want to pass out somewhere.*

I made my way over to the edge of the park to a small wall. I peered over the wall down a steep rocky cliff face. I spotted a ledge about 100 feet down that was dark and in the shadows. I followed along the wall and found a small path leading down to the ledge. It was dark, old beer cans littered the large smooth stones on the ledge. I laid out my sleeping bag as close to the face of the cliff as possible. There was a bike path that ran the perimeter of the park up above; I wanted to be out of view.

I knotted my boots together and secured them to my backpack. They were my most valuable resource after my passport, which I shoved down my pants. I used the rope from my sleeping bag to secure my backpack to the bag, and climbed in. I lay there, with the rocks protruding into my back and shoulders, and drifted off to sleep to the sound of the ocean.

21 HOMELESS, MAN

Day 40 December 17th

I awoke to the sun beating down on my face, my body dripping sweat inside my sleeping bag. As I sat up, the blood drained down from my head. Extremely lightheaded, and fatigued, I looked down to see my sleeping bag completely covered in dust. *It's hot. I'm thirsty*, my body began complaining. *No you're not. Let's head back up to the park before anyone comes down here.*

I went to put on my boots. *Why is this so difficult?* One boot on. I struggled to put my foot into the other, using all my might. Two boots on. *Small victory.* My body didn't want to do a single thing. I sat there on my bag for a few minutes – boots on. Very slowly, I rolled my sleeping bag and climbed up the path toward the park, taking multiple breaks along the way. *Everything seems like a huge task right now… It's your energy. You need to eat something.*

I sat there on a bench analyzing my remaining rations – a few handfuls of Ica nuts, an avocado, and ¾ of a pancito. I had about 16 oz of clean water from a water bottle a devotee gifted me back in Cusco. *It's Sunday morning. Your flight is on Wednesday – with a layover in Mexico City – you won't be in Dallas until Thursday. This has to last you the next 5 days,* I reminded myself.

Overlooking the ocean, I sat and enjoyed my avocado and pancito. Still dealing with stomach sickness, I prayed my body would metabolize the food. With low energy, I sat there napping under a tree for the entirety of the day, until the sun began to set.

The wind picked up and the temperature dropped, signaling me it was time to get up and move. I made my way the few blocks over to Kennedy Park. I noticed there was large crowd gathered around, watching and clapping, as people danced in the center. I pushed my way into the group, surrounding myself with bodies to block the gusts of wind. I stood there for about two hours, staying warm with the other bodies around me. It was nice to watch people have fun; it kept my mind off of the weather, food, and my sleeping situation. But even better, I didn't feel so alone, even if it was just for a few minutes. When the dancing was over, I was back to wondering the streets of Mira Flores.

I returned to the nearby shopping mall to brush my teeth and take shelter before it closed. Alone, tired, and hungry, I stood there staring like a zombie at the TV's. I just stared at an 82-inch

Ultra High Def Plasma TV as pictures of perfectly plated food, salads and fruits came across the screen. Then I would turn around and watch the 60-inch plasma with pictures of the Himalayan Mountains and the New York City skyline.

"Excuse me. Sir. Excuse me. We're closing."

I nodded, and made my way back down the escalator, out the sliding doors, and into the windy night.

Slowly, I made my way back to the park and crawled down to the secret terrace. I secured my belongings before drifting off to sleep…

December 18th

Day 41

Wow. It's hot. Your face is gonna peel if you keep laying here. Come on. Let's pack and get up to the shade. I sat up. My body no longer wanted to respond to the commands I was giving it.

Good theory, the moving and all that, but it may take a bit. What's wrong with you? Why are you moving so slowly, why aren't you listening to me?

Because I need food! I have traveler's sickness, and all you're giving me is a few Ica nuts.

Eventually, I managed to get my shoes on and my bag rolled up. And step-by-step, I made my way up the path to my spot under the tree in the park, overlooking the ocean. I pulled out the Ica nuts.

I am so thankful I have these right now. I sat there looking at the small bean shaped nuts in the palm of my hand. Ica nuts were different than other nuts I had eaten in the past. They had a texture similar to cardboard, and my body had a hard time breaking down the fat and fiber. I would eat a few and I could feel them sitting in my stomach for hours. They would give me a stomachache and make me tired. However, it was fuel, and I was alive.

I laid there under the tree, dozing in and out, my body wanting to move as little as possible. As the sunset, I again made my way to Kennedy Park, to the mall to layer up and brush my teeth. Tonight it wasn't too cold, Thank God. It was back down to the terrace for the 3rd night.

December 19th

Day 42 Tuesday.

Ah, that sun in bright! It's OK. Your flight is tomorrow. Today we walk to Lima.

I laid there covered in dust on the rocks of the terrace, not moving. Slowly, very slowly I packed. The trail up to the park became a trek of its own. I made it back under my tree for breakfast. I had been light on my rations, about a cup of nuts remained and about 4 ounces of water. I sipped and snacked before beginning the return trek to Lima.

As I left the park in Mira Flores, I was stopped and greeted by a fellow traveler, an older man about 50 years old, heavy set, wearing a Hawaiian style shirt, which rested on his belly.

"Hello! My friend! My friend!" the man called and waved me over.

Hmm… this is how I greeted drivers when I asked them for rides after waiting for hours on the side of the road. This man is in desperation mode.

"Hey, what's up?"

"My friend, my friend, I need your help."

The man had just flown in from the Netherlands for a two-week vacation. On his cab ride from the airport to Mira Flores, the cab driver dropped him off and robbed him of his entire belongings –all of his bags, passport, wallet everything. He had contacted the embassy, and they had given him a hotel for 2 nights until they could get him a new passport to get home.

"I'm screwed! I have no money, nothing! Everything is gone," the man began weeping. "Can you please spare me some money, anything to help me get food and live for the next few days?"

I could feel his fear and desperation. Feelings I had become so familiar with these past few weeks.

I smiled. "Hey! You're gonna be alright, man."

The man was weeping and wiping his tears.

"Look. Look. You're gonna be alright. I can't give you any money. I don't have any money, but don't worry, man. Trust me, you're going to live. "

"You have no money? What? You have been robbed also?" asked the man.

"No. No. This is the last day of a 6-week trip. I didn't bring money with me."

"You didn't bring money! Why? Why would you do that?"

"No. No money, but I'm all right. Listen, you don't need as much as you think you do. Your brain wants to freak out. Just trust me, you will be taken care of. Don't worry. Here. I do have these."

I pulled the bag of Ica nuts from my backpack.

"These will keep you alive for the next few days."

"What? Don't you need them?"

"My flight is tomorrow. I will have more food when I get home. Look, you have a hotel, and you've got some food. You'll be alright, man."

The man immediately began digging into the nuts.

"Just a heads up, they're pretty dense, I wouldn't eat them all at one time. Lots of calories though, they'll keep you alive."

"Thank you. Thank you."

We hugged, and I continued my trek to Lima.

My energy during the trek was extremely low. I stopped multiple times to sit and recharge. The afternoon sun was hot, directly overhead. As I walked the sidewalks, there was little shade. I was down to my last few ounces of water, which I was saving for the trek to the airport.

Water. Water. Water. It was all I could think about. Every time I passed a corner store or a food cart on the street, I couldn't help but stare down the bottles of water.

By mid afternoon, I was back in Lima at the same park where I had met the girl who wanted to be an actress in LA. I found a large tree providing shade from the sun, removed my shoes, and enjoyed a nice nap. *Tomorrow you're flying home.*

Awake from my nap, I rested there, relaxed and carefree, contemplating my next move. *It's your last night, your last night. Are you just gonna stay here at the park and roll out your sleeping bag? Maybe.* The grass was a bit softer than the stones on the terrace. *Maybe you can just pull an all-nighter? Ehh, that could be fun, but I don't think I have the energy.*

What about the temple? We're not too far away- maybe they'll let you crash there since your flight is tomorrow. No harm in asking.

I watched the sun set, grabbed my bag, and made my way over to the temple. At the front desk was my friend Edgar, the Mr. Smee doppelganger.

"Ah! Michael! You are back!

"Si."

"How was Cusco?"

"Amazing. It was perfect."

"You .. want to sleep here tonight, at the temple?

"Yes, that would be awesome."

"Ok, Ok, I go ask the commander."

A few minutes later they returned.

"Yes. Yes. Michael. You stay tonight!"

They welcomed me in, leading me back to the closet and up the ladder to the hidden devotee loft to place my bag. Up in the loft was a new devotee, Camila, who I hadn't met before.

"Prasada?" he asked.

"Si. Pero. Quiero ayudar," I want to help I explained.

"Despues, Despues." He told me

We went back to the kitchen, and he served me a small bowl of potatoes with a mysterious looking, creamy, orange sauce.

"Muchas Gracias"

I stared down at the bowl. I said my prayer

and took a bite. *Dude, take it easy. I know you've only been eating a few nuts, but take it easy,* my stomach warned me. I continued eating, not wanting to be rude, but my stomach was rejecting it. I finished the potatoes.

"What can I do? I want to help."

I took out the restaurant trash and washed the dishes that were piling up in the sink of the restaurant. *The food. The food wasn't sitting well in my stomach.*

I rushed to the bathroom and up it came. *Damn. You needed that fuel. You have a long trek to the airport tomorrow,* my body reminded me.

I retired up to the loft, my sleeping bag spread out over a yoga mat on the wooden floor - a bit cozier than the rocks of the terrace. *Thank you for this shelter.*

22 PANETÓN DANCE

Day 43 December 20th

I heard Camila get out of bed. The loft was pitch black.

"Que hora es?" I asked my new friend.

"4:30. I go to temple wake up deity. You want to come?"

"Si. Si."

Why not? It's your last day in Peru.

I made my way upstairs to the temple room. Beautiful paintings and murals covered the walls and a massive, awe inspiring alter to Krishna stood in the front.

After my morning meditation, I packed and prepared to hit the road. I went through my bag and gifted Camila my Under Armor shirt and a pair of shorts. In return he gave me a hand knitted, winter cap, with llamas on it.

"Prasada? Breakfast?" Asked Camila

"Si. Gracias. Muchas, gracias."

I knew I had to leave by 10:30. It had taken me about 4 hours to walk downtown from the airport my first day.

Back in the devotee kitchen, Camila offered me a banana, a fresh hand made tortilla, and bread. On the table was a dipping sauce made from blended almonds, red pepper, and salt. I sat there staring down the bounty before me, and Camila walked over with a metal mug.

"Hot cocoa," he said with a smile.

Oh Hellllllll yes.

As we were eating, a devotee entered with a plate of prasada that had been offered that morning to the deity. There were three kinds of sweets, dulce. One was a banana and brown sugar mash that I spread on a piece of the bread. The combination reminded me of my mother's banana bread, a little slice of home.

After breakfast, I did the dishes and cleaned the kitchen for the devotees. I went around the temple to say my good-byes. Before I left, Camila asked me to chant a mantra with him for protection:

"Narashimha
Maha Mantra:

Ugram Veeram
Maka Vishnum
Juralantham
Sharvato Mukham
Nrisimham
Bheesharam Bhadram
Mrityu Mrityum
Namaam Taham"

He gave it to me written on a piece of paper to keep. It was time to hit the road.

Now a veteran, I wrapped a shirt around my face to block the sun, leaving space for my nose and eyes. It was a scorching day. High energy from the cocoa, I spent the walk reflecting on my journey, every step, getting closer to the airport, closer to home. A few miles into the trip, I couldn't help but think of water. *Aqua water. Necesito water.* I began doing anything I could to keep my mind off of water, knowing that my next water would come from a flight attendant on the flight. I was getting close, so close. I entered this weird state of mind, so filled with joy - I started singing Feliz Navidad, chanting Hare Krishna, and doing a little dance every time I saw a person carrying a bag of Panetón, in my mind I called it the "Panetón dance." I was losing my mind, maybe, but I was blissed out, dehydrated, and amped up on some cacao. I kept walking, fantasizing about hugging my mother again, seeing my family, crushing some of her famous poppy seed bread on Christmas morning. *Blink and you'll be there*, I reminded myself.

As I kept walking, I spotted the airplanes taking off, getting closer and closer. Then I spotted a sign in the distance, "Aeropuerto 5km." "Areopuerto!" I began chanting out loud as I continued through the streets, step by step. Before I knew it - there I was, walking back through those same sliding doors, into the airport. *You did it.*

I arrived at the airport at 2 in the afternoon, scanning the lobby for AeroMexico. Nope. Nothing. I checked the last page of my notebook. Written there, in black ink:

"Departing flight Dec 20 4:50PM
AeroMexico Confirmation # OSFKLY"

Shit. I really hope I didn't mess this up. What if they changed the flight? What if you wrote the wrong date? How can there be no AeroMexico?
Well dude, if you had your phone you could check your e-mail. Maybe they changed the flight and tried contacting you. A lot can happen in 6 weeks.

I found someone who worked at the airport

"Donde Aero Mexico?"

"Gate 30- en la tarde" instructing me it would change later in the afternoon.

I took a seat and began writing in my journal. A few minutes later, I looked up to see the blue and white sign on the monitor in front of me,

AeroMexico. *Yes! We're goin' home.*

After security, I walked past the newsstands selling bottles of water. *Water… Water… Close… So close.*

It was still a bit early so I found a seat at a neighboring gate with windows and less of a crowd. I sat there staring out the window watching the planes take off, reflecting. The woman sitting next to me sparked up a conversation. She had just finished her vacation and was returning to Italy. We talked about Europe and her favorite cities in Italy. She was describing Venice to me when I heard over the intercom, "Michael Mcgloogin please report to gate 21." *Shit. Shit. No. You're gonna miss your flight. No way, it's only 4:30.*

"Michael Mcgloogin?"

"Yes, yes I'm here"

"We almost closed the gate. We were waiting for you."

"My ticket says 4:50."

"The flight was moved forward."

"Lo siento," I said smiling, happy that I made it.

Sheeeeit. That was a close call.

I found my seat and settled in. I couldn't wipe the smile from my face.

As I sat there in that comfortable chair, I

couldn't believe it was coming to an end. I began to reflect back to first landing in Lima, first leaving the airport. All the times I wanted to give up and just go home. *You made it 6 weeks in a foreign country with no money, no friends, no phone, no plans- Blink and it's over.* It felt like a dream, like it didn't happen, yet it felt like an entire lifetime.

All of these thoughts and emotions were a bit overwhelming. I was so grateful to be alive, to be back on the plane.

"Excuse me sir, would you like a refreshment?" *An angel. It was another angel, dressed as a flight attendant.*

"Si, si. Aqua. Water. Muchas Gracias."

I watched as the woman poured a crystal clear stream from the bottle into the cup. She handed it to me. I held the cup up to my mouth wrapping my dry, cracked lips around the rim. I felt the moisture touch my lips. I couldn't stop drinking. I finished the cup in a few gulps..

"Gracias" I handed her my cup, "Can I have a bit more please?"

Again, I slugged down the refreshing liquid.

"More?" she joked.

I smiled, "Yes, por favor." The third cup I was able to enjoy a bit more.

The flight attendant came around with snack bags of peanuts and dinner. A small, Styrofoam cup of lettuce and some pasta noodles with a red watery sauce.

No meat, No dairy. Thank God. I'm spoiled - Sitting on this comfy plane, eating some fine Italian cuisine.

I landed in Mexico City with a 10-hour layover. After customs, I found a wall near one of the boarding gates and whipped out my sleeping bag. *10hrs... No problem. We're gonna catch up on some sleep. Look at this giant shelter.* Sheltered from the elements, laying on a flat surface, I quickly dozed off and slept like a baby.

23 HOWDY,

Day 44 December 21ˢᵗ

Rise and Shine. *Oh, no! No! Not again…my stomach.* I hopped up, rapidly rolled my sleeping bag, and bolted through the airport looking for the bathroom. My body still wasn't absorbing the energy from food.

It had been a week since I had left the Temple at Cusco - 7 days of hitching and walking over 674 miles. The past few days I had only consumed a few Ica nuts, except for the breakfast in Lima and the noodles on the plane.

I boarded the flight to Dallas, and sat in my chair, staring out the window, fantasizing about food. After we took off, the flight attendant came around with the meal - ham and cheese on a buttery croissant with yogurt. *Don't cave now. You're almost back.* I stared at my neighbor's croissant...

Are you gonna die?

Are you gonna die if you don't eat right now?

No? Alright then.

I kept dozing off on the flight to Dallas. My body just wanted to stay in shut down mode.

"Passengers, please prepare for landing," came over the speakers. It was 10 AM, and I had made it back to the United States. I did my best to stay excited, but physically, I was feeling like absolute shit. It was the worst my body had felt the whole trip.

Alright, alright, alright. Let's do this. We're almost home.

There I was at DFW. Only having my backpack as a carry on, I was able to cut through the Quick-Check customs.

In a bit of a haze. I made my way up to the desk.

"Can I have your paper?"

"Paper?..." I looked around.

"Yes, your paper, can you hand it to me?"

"...Paper?... Passport?"

"Hey man, you alright?" the guy asked

"Yeah, I'm fine. What's up?"

"I need your customs paper."

"Customs paper?"

He pointed behind me at the rows of computers and giant signs saying to print out a custom paper.

Ahhh… I see…

"Ah.. my bad man, I didn't even see them."

"You didn't see them? You sure you're alright man?

"Yeah. Yeah. I'm fine"

I walked back to the machine to print out the paper… *It's frozen. Damn the machine is frozen. He's gonna think its you. He's just staring over at you. I'm hitting the button. I'm hitting the button! It's frozen.*

"Sir, Sir, do you need assistance? Do you need me to call someone?"

"No, it's not me. It's the machine."

Come on. Come on.

Finally! It printed.

"Here. Here. I have it," I handed him the sheet at the counter.

"Where are you coming from?"

"Lima"

"Alright. Take care of yourself now."

Walking out to the lobby, I was thinking about how I was going to navigate through Dallas without currency or a phone. *This is it. You just need a map of Dallas. You did Peru. This will be easy.*

"Hey there, Can I help you with something?" an older, black woman behind the information desk greeted me with a southern accent.

"Uh.. Yeah, actually…Do you have a map of Dallas?"

"A map! Honey, don't you have a phone on you that you could use or something?"

"Nope. Not on me. I just need a map."

"I'm not too sure we have any of those lying around. Where are you trying to get to?"

"My sisters place. She lives on Belmont Ave. Do you know where that is?"

"The name sounds familiar, but I don't know exactly. Hey, are you by yourself?

"Yeah."

"Traveling alone with no phone?"

"Yes."

"… Not the sharpest tool in the shed."

"Thanks. Do you know how to get downtown at least? I can figure it out from there."

"Well… You've got a few options. You can take the bus, or a cab, or the metro."

"No. I'm going to walk. Do you know the best

route?"

"Walk! Oh no honey. You can't walk downtown! You'll get yourself killed. It's all highways. You must be out your mind."

"I know. I know. If you don't have a map, it's ok. I'll figure something out. Thanks."

"Hold on crazy boy. Let me see if I can find you something."

The woman returned with a small tourist guide to Dallas - one of those little magazines with restaurants and advertisements, and a pamphlet on airport transportation.

"There's a few small maps in here," she said, handing me the magazine.

"Thank you. Thank you."

"Seriously honey, I wouldn't walk from here."

I just smiled, "Thank you for the map," and walked away.

I sat on the bench flipping through the pages.. *Damn. Dallas is huge. Downtown.. Uptown.. Belmont.. Belmont.. Belmont… Boom! Belmont Ave, Uptown...* From the other map, I could see that there was a major highway, route 114, going straight from the airport to downtown. *From the airport hitch downtown, from there you can walk to uptown.* I had a plan.

The woman walked over to the bench, "Do

you want me to call your parents or something?"

"No. No. I'm fine thank you," laughing.

"Here, at least take this water, you crazy boy." She handed me an 8oz mini bottle.

"Thank you!"

"Be safe now. Can you at least give me your parent's number so I can tell them that I saw you? You know, in case something happens…"

"No. No, thanks. I'm alright. Thank you. "

What is everyone so scared of?

I began walking out of the airport, following the signs for the airport exit, Once I passed the drop off area, the sidewalk disappeared so I continued on the shoulder. I walked along the shoulder. The road turned into a 4-lane highway and the shoulder disappeared, leaving me walking along the white line. Cars zipped right past me from behind.

Shit. That was close. That was really close. Maybe this wasn't the best idea. These cars were flying by. I could feel the surge of wind blast me every time. *Your body, this human vessel, is no match for a large mass of metal flying at 70mph. This isn't smart, kid.*

Stop. Stop. No. There's nothing to be scared of. You're a pro, man. You just hitchhiked all over Peru. Just do your thing.

Well here goes nothing… First hitch in the U.S….

As I walked down the Airport exit, I had this weird sense of confidence. I put my thumb up, smiling. The cars continued to zip by as I walked with my thumb up. A few honks, mostly just looks of shock and confusion.

A van pulled off about 20 yards ahead. There were numbers on the back of the windshield. *Shit, it's a cab.* I continued walking as I waved him off, signaling him to continue on. He didn't move. I kept waving him off as I neared the van.

He rolled down his window.

"Sorry man, I didn't know you were a cab," I kept walking.

"Where are you going?"

"I don't need a cab man, thanks." *These guys are persistent*, I thought.

"You're going to get yourself killed out here."

"Thanks man, I'm good," I continued walking with my thumb up.

"Hey! Where are you going?"

"I'm just trying to hitch a ride out of the airport to the main road 35E or 114 that heads into downtown."

"Hop in. I'll take you to the road, then it's a straight shot to downtown."

"I don't have money, man. I can just hitch

another ride."

"Just hop in it's a few minutes down the road. You can't walk this."

"Thanks."

I hopped in the black van. The driver was from Iraq, 35 years old and looking for a wife. He dropped me off at a gas station a few minutes down the road.

"This isn't the highway, but it runs parallel. Just walk straight. You've got a hell of a journey ahead of you."

"Thanks man."

It was about 11 AM when I left the cab. I started my way down the road towards downtown Dallas, passing a Whole Foods, a massive strip mall, and a bank all on the same block. It was a little different scenery than Peru. *Let's hitch, why not.*

I stood across the street from the Whole Foods parking lot, in front of a bank with my thumb up. A few minutes went by. Hundreds, and hundreds of cars were passing through this intersection. Range Rovers, Mercedes - most of the vehicles were empty except for the driver. Large SUVs, Chevy Tahoe's, with 7 open seats, cruising right past me. Most people were blowing by, pre-occupied, not even noticing. Some people laughed and honked as they passed. Some people stared, confused, almost scared. Then there were those that shot looks of disgust and pity. *Come on lets move.*

I walked and I walked and I walked and I walked and I walked…. And I walked … and I walked… and I started feeling extremely tired, and worn out, and hungry, and thirsty, so I found a spot in the shade, under a tree on the side of the road and I napped.

Come on. We're so close. We're in Dallas. Just keep moving. You can't lie here anymore, at least try to hitch. I stood there on the side of the road, in front of a church with my thumb high in the air. Car, after car, after car, blew by. No dice. Just a few more laughs and dirty looks.

I had been walking south for miles, and I knew I had miles and miles ahead of me. Any distance would be amazing - even just a few blocks. I stopped on a corner next to a stoplight. A woman stopped at the light in a white SUV with her window down.

"Excuse me ma'am, are you heading south?" I pointed straight ahead in the direction her vehicle was facing.

She just looked at me.

Clearly we both knew the answer to that question.

"Can I ride with you for a few blocks? I'm heading downtown."

"No. No. No, Sorry."

I waited for the next red light. A car pulled up with

the windows down, blasting southern rap.

"Hey! Are you guys headed south toward downtown?"

They stared.

"Are you going downtown?"

"Nah, Nah, man."

Cool. Cool, Man.

Well.. that went well. Any other brilliant ideas?

The quote from Dr Seuss popped in my head.

"You have brains in your head. You have feet
in your shoes. You can steer yourself any
direction you choose. You're on your own.
And you know what you know. And YOU are
the one who'll decide where to go."

*Come on baby. You're in Dallas. It's the last stretch.
You don't need a ride. We're gonna get there. We're
gonna walk.*

So I walked, and I walked, and I walked, and I walked. More luxury vehicles and SUVs passed me by. I walked past strip malls, and shopping centers, and bank, after bank, after bank, after restaurant, after strip mall, after shopping center, after bank, after country club, and restaurants, and luxury shops. Then came the mansions, fortresses dressed up with dazzling, magnificent Christmas light displays. Each one taking up an entire block.

The excess was smacking me in the face as I walked past another country club with a row of mansions across the street. I thought back to my walk through Cañete - the shacks, the clay huts, the dwellings made of plywood and metal, the stray dogs, and the cornfields.

I kept walking and walking as the sun went down. I looked around me - more fortresses fenced in with massive walls, guarding the pools and guesthouses in the back. *Well, at least I can literally sleep anywhere tonight and feel safe. Just hop a wall, roll out my sleeping bag. I'll be set.*

Then the road forked. I recognized a street name from my trip to Dallas the summer before. I pulled out the map in the advertising pamphlet. I couldn't tell the scale or distance, but I knew it was the right direction. My location was now visible on the map, no more walking blind. I turned down Fitzhugh Ave.

The sun had set. I had no idea what time it was or how long I had been walking. *Don't worry about it. It's nighttime and you'll get there when you get there- sometime tonight.*

I continued walking and walking, past an Equinox, more strip malls, restaurants, and cycling places, more mansions and mini mansions. I continued trekking until I came to a major highway.

Looking across the overpass, I spotted a coffee shop that looked vaguely familiar. *Aha! It's the coffee shop you stopped at with Mom last summer.*

You're close, oh, you're so close.

A giant grin came across my face.

"Alright, Alright, Alright," I said aloud.

I continued down the road. This was it - LA to Peru to Dallas. *You did it.*

Belmont Ave. There I was, standing outside her apartment complex- shut out by the gate.

So close. So close.

I was there, but I was stuck.

It's fine. It's fine.

The gate opened to let a car escape. I walked into the parking lot.

Yes!

No.

Shit.

Another gate blocked the stairwell.

I spotted a woman sitting in a pick up truck double parked near the entrance to the stairwell with her windows down. I approached the car and saw her staring down at her phone.

"Excuse me ma'am," I greeted her.

She jumped back. I had clearly surprised her, pulling her from SnapChat.

"Can I borrow your phone for a second? My sister lives here. I just need to call her quick to let me in."

She looked at me like I asked her to sacrifice her first born child.

"My phone? You want to use MY phone?" I could see her grip it a bit tighter, "You don't...You don't have one?"

"No, not on me... It's a long story."

She sat there staring at me, gripping her device.

"You know what... It's cool. Forget about it. It's cool."

I turned to walk away just as a man exited the gate.

"Can you hold that? Thanks man."

I climbed the flights of stairs, double checked the apartment number in my notebook, and knocked.

Yes, barking... It's Dex. The door opened... my sister stood there in front of me. I embraced her in my arms... I was home.

CLOSING

I do not have all of the answers for you, but I was lucky to learn a few lessons throughout my journey.

I discovered that money is not necessary for life. It can't warm you up like a fire, it can't quench your thirst like a sip of water, nor can it fill your belly like a loaf of fresh bread. It can't hug you when you're lonely, nor can it shelter you from the wind or the rain. It is a symbol. A symbol we choose to believe in. As a symbol, it only has the power we give it.

It seems that there is a force that binds us and connects us all. It being the strongest, purest force in this existence. Energy is real. We need energy to live. Even if you have nothing, no physical possessions, no money– you still have something you can give, in the form of energy. The universe will use your natural gifts – a word of wisdom, inspiration, English lessons, physical labor, even cooking. Whatever it is that you have to give, you can give it, and you will be rewarded. "Give and ye shall receive."

I realized that I was more powerful than I had ever imagined, and that this world has underlying laws like gravity that you won't find in science textbooks. One of the biggest lessons learned from this experience was this simple truth:

I have everything I need.

A special thank you to the Hare Krishna Temples in Lima, Eco Truly, Cusco, and the Sacred Valley and to all the devotees and volunteers who shared their energy with me throughout my journey.

Muchas Gracias,

Allí – there
Almuerzo – lunch
Amor - love
Aqui – here
Ayer - yesterday
Ayudar – to help
Bien – good
Boleto – ticket
Bueno - good
Caminar – to walk
Carne- meat
Carro – Car/ Truck
Casa – home/room
Cocina - kitchen
Come – eat
Comer- to eat
Como estas? - How
are you?
Compañero – buddy/
sidekick / friend
Cuando – When
Cuantos – how
many?
Descanso – rest
Direcciones -
directions
Donde – Where
Dormir – to sleep
Esta bien –It's ok
Esta noche – tonight

Estoy bien – I am
good
Frío - cold
Hablar – to speak
hablas – do you
speak?
hermano- brother
Horas – hours
La finca – the farm
Limpiar – to clean
Mas – more
Mochila – back pack
Muchas Gracias –
thank you very much
Necesitas – you need
Necesito – I need
No entiendo – I don't
understand
No puedo – I cant
No se – I don't know
Nunca - never
Pan/Pancito – bread
Para – for
Peligroso –
dangerous
Pero – but
Poco – little bit
Pollo – Chicken
Por Que? – Why?
Puedo – I can/ Can I?

Que? – What?

Queso – cheese

Quiero – I want

Químicos - chemicals

Sabado – Saturday

Salir – exit/ leave

Semana – week

Sur - South

Tarde – later

Tengo – I have

Toro - Bull

Trabajar – to work

Va – to go

Vamos – We go

Vamos – we go /
come on

Verdad - True

Viaje – travel

Visitar – to visit

Voy – I go

Made in the USA
Middletown, DE
05 January 2021